THE
Strange Paths
WE ALL FOLLOW

Table of Contents

Special Thanks..i
Introduction...iii
Chapter 1...1
    Last Dance with the Devil..........................1
Chapter 2...8
    A Sad Love Story..8
Chapter 3..11
    Death of Innocence..11
Chapter 4..14
    Third Time's a Charm....................................14
Chapter 5..19
    Hang 'em High..19
Chapter 6..25
    Something Out of the Ordinary...................25
Chapter 7..32
    Poopy Pants Bandit.......................................32
Chapter 8..35
    Side Quests for Everyone............................35
Chapter 9..38
    Ross. From Friends.......................................38
Chapter 10..42
    Backpack Full of Smiles..............................42
Chapter 11..46
    The Beautiful Mistakes We All Make.........46
Chapter 12..50
    Always Lawyer Up..50
Chapter 13..53
    The Sh*t You Can Buy on eBay...................53
Chapter 14..63
    Weenie Roasting Furries.............................63
Chapter 15..68
    Fly Me to the Moon......................................68
Chapter 16..74
    No Need for Batteries..................................74

Chapter 17	80
Divorced at 23, 29, and 36	80
Chapter 18	85
Laughter From Beyond	85
Chapter 19	88
The Seers	88
Chapter 20	90
Proceed with Extreme Caution	90
Chapter 21	92
What Gets Spent in Vegas	92
Chapter 22	98
I Met a Ghost	98
Chapter 23	107
Fortunate Wanderer	107
Chapter 24	118
Madame Vera	118
Dedication	123
Acknowledgements	125
About the author	127

Special Thanks

This is my first attempt at writing a book. I really appreciate every single one of you that took the time and spent the money to read this. I hope my story will inspire you, educate you, and of course entertain you. Thank you very much.

Introduction

When I first set out to write this book, I never thought it would make it this far. I figured it would be a few short stories for my kids to read when they were old enough. Not so much because I wanted to leave a legacy, but because I've lived through some crazy stuff. I want to not only show them just how nuts it can all get, but how spectacular it can be as well. I hope they are able to find some sort of lesson in it and maybe live a little better because of it.

What ended up happening is the book that you hold in your hands. More than I expected, probably because even *I* was unaware of everything I had been through until I started telling it.

And, as I told the stories, I came to realize that life is a treasure. I saw just how much I had been through, and all that had almost happened. The times I had been blessed, cursed, and the recipient of pure dumb luck. And, I thought, maybe someone else might like to read this.

Well congratulations, reader, because you now have in your hands one of the strangest lives I have ever had the privilege to live, and I am glad to have you along for the ride.

"There's blood on the walls when Charlie and the family make house calls." —Ozzy Osbourne

Chapter 1

Last Dance with the Devil

Sometimes, you don't even know how close you've come to the abyss. Pain, terror, or worse can be something that you brush up against without even knowing it. I had one of those fleeting encounters when I was just eight years old, and the experience still sends shivers down my spine.

The three of us were coming home from the gym, late one Wednesday night after having fun. It was the eighties and the media's flaunting of serial killers and child molesters hadn't quite gotten a stranglehold on our collective imagination yet. In the town I lived in, a small northwestern bedroom community in the heart of the Rockies, serial killers were a rarity. The town had a grand total of 60,000 people. We were a pretty tight knit, if somewhat relaxed, sort of community. We left our doors unlocked and didn't really have to worry about a lot of crime.

It was just after 9:00 PM, and the teacher watching us at open gym had finally kicked us out to go home. What little homework we were given had been done hours before. We were heading home to go to bed. It was an October night and the sun had already gone down, leaving the streets lit up by the dim, sporadically placed street lamps that stood on the street corners.

My friend Jim and I were joking with each other and talking while Jim's little brother bounced around in his typical, annoying little brother sort of way, chattering at us and to himself. He was young, easily excited, and usually ignored.

So, when he pointed in the distance and said, "What is that guy doing?" we did what we usually did. We just kept on walking. In fact, the only reason I can even remember it in hindsight is probably because of just how bizarre the whole night turned out.

It was dark out, and that particular stretch of road didn't have any light at all except for the occasional house porch. Our houses were only ten minutes away, and we knew the walk pretty well. Jim and I kept talking, and might not have noticed anything if we hadn't plowed into the back of his stopped little brother.

"What's going on?" Jim started in on him. His fuse was never quite as short as it was when dealing with his brother.

He would have really gotten after him too if he hadn't said suddenly, "Did you guys see that guy?" Fear had crept up into his voice, raising his little boy timbre into little more than a squeak. A shaky hand slowly lifted up, pointing farther down the road.

The black night sky darkened the shadows as the three of us stopped in our tracks, straining our eyes in the direction of his wavering finger. A few seconds ticked tensely by as we waited for the figure he had seen. Ten seconds later, Jim was turning to tease his brother when I saw the movement.

"Look!" I whispered.

Sure enough, the hunched figure of a man could just barely be seen running across the road from an empty duplex to hide behind a big pine tree.

The three of us stood there in silence, trying to figure out what to do next. Our houses were about three blocks away, but this guy was about a block and a half from us... and right where we needed to go.

Like some kind of strange horror movie, we did the only thing we could think to do: we walked towards him. After all, what could go wrong? It was probably just one of the neighbors thinking to give us a good scare anyway.

When we got within twenty-five feet or so of where he was, the figure finally came out from behind the evergreen with a bright flashlight shining in our faces.

"Ha-ha, Mike," we said. "We totally saw you hiding earlier." We were making the assumption that it was our friend's, who did not come with us that night, dad. He liked to play practical jokes on us. This was a little out of character but you never knew with him. We kept walking forward but the person, whoever it was, didn't say anything. He had his flashlight trained right on our eyes, keeping us from seeing who he was. When he still didn't say anything, we all started to get the feeling like something was wrong.

Jim stopped cold. His brother actually took off running backwards. For whatever stupid reason I had in my head, my feet kept walking forward until I was within five feet of this figure whom I desperately hoped was someone I knew.

He was tall. Six feet at least. I could vaguely make out a blue jacket, but his face was too close to the flashlight for me to get a good look. I looked down and saw a detail that has stuck with me my whole life. He was no one I knew. I had never seen this face, even though it was terribly dark out and the features were hard to define. Still. I knew.

The nerve that had steeled me long enough to walk this close suddenly failed and, as terror engulfed me, I ran. Nearly the same time, the man's hand reached out to grab me before I could flee, grazing the back of my head as my fear-driven legs started pumping down the street in the opposite direction. "Run!" came a scream, forcing its way out of me towards my friends who were already well aware of the predicament we were in.

We took a side road to the left and kept running until we saw a woman getting groceries out of her car. When she saw us, like three bats out of hell, she called out, "Hey, kids!"

Her voice carried through the cold night air, stopping our pursuer at the corner. To this day I truly believe that was our angel. There to protect us as it was not our time to leave this earth.

The one thing that stood out, that I will never forget, as I looked back to what I thought was a predator about to catch me, was that in that iridescent glow of the lone street lamp was the lower half of the man that was chasing us. He just stood there at the corner of the intersecting roads we just ran from and the only really concrete memory I had was that he was wearing white pants.

A few more houses down and we were pounding and screaming like banshees on the door of one of the town's cops. He listened to us and stuck his head out the door. But our stalker had left the street corner, returning to his shadows.

In the days that followed, we asked around as to who it could have been. None of our neighbors would admit to the prank, even years after the fact. But, in questioning, I did come across a strange incident that made me wonder who we had run into.

All the way home

So almost twenty years to the date of the incident described above, I found myself at a family reunion. My sister, whom I hadn't seen in a while due to her living out of state for many years, was back in town. Fun was always to be had when she was back.

Sometime near the end of one of the nights, we found ourselves by our lonesome and in a deep conversation of recollection. In my tired stupor, I remembered the story of my possible run-in with a kidnapper. I always wanted to ask her about our time growing up on Valley View street. So I did.

"So when we were growing up, did you ever experience anything weird in our neighborhood or around where we lived?" I then proceeded to tell her of my experience. She initially said that nothing came to mind. Although, when I mentioned the one vivid detail I could and always will remember, it sparked a look in her. And here is what she told me:

My sister was fourteen at the time, putting this night about two years before we had our run-in.

At the time, she regularly babysat for neighbors when they wanted to have a night out, and the job had just come to an end. The baby was put to bed and the parents had just arrived, drunk. They were starting to make awkward advances toward each other, making my sister a little uncomfortable.

"Do you want a ride home?" the father asked, slightly slurring his speech.

"No thanks," my sister replied, "It's just a five-minute walk. I'll be fine." His wife came out of the back room with some cash and handed it to her, thanking her as she walked out the door.

The night was a cool, clear summer night and the moon was shining bright. Traffic had finally died down and she walked home in the moonlight, unafraid. Friday nights were a great time to be out, and it was beautiful. My sister didn't have a care in the world. That is, until she heard the steps behind her.

She glanced back and saw a man walking behind her, slowly drawing closer. It's ok, she thought. Lots of people walk outside on Friday nights. But, just in case, she picked up her pace a little bit.

And so did the person behind her.

She walked faster and faster, but each time the man behind her matched her speed.

I'll turn up here she thought, onto our street, and that will be the end of that. Won't you feel stupid? She tried to chide herself. But when she made the turn, he did too. She broke out into a run, hoping that she could make it into the house before he caught up to her and the steps behind her started pounding the pavement, gaining on her.

When she finally burst through the front door of the house, my dad jumped to his feet. "Someone... was chasing me," she managed to get out between heavy breaths. But, when my dad looked outside, no one was there. My sister slowly calmed herself, trying to convince herself that she was okay. There couldn't have been anyone out there, she tried to reason with herself. Dad hadn't seen anyone, had he? Well dad is a little drunk too came the little voice in her head.

He went around locking up the doors while my sister slowed her breathing and started to relax. My sister decided to go out to the front bay window of our house. Just to calm herself down and tell herself she was just paranoid.

"You know what clicked for me when you told me the story about you and your friends' run-in? It was that lasting image you had. You see, I had gone to the front window to alleviate my fears but they only arose further. Because there, on the corner of our street and the street that led south to my old elementary school, was the guy who was behind me. Standing there. And the one thing I could see off the light of his cigarette was the white of his pants."

Homework for you

Wiki, Google, do whatever search or searches you want on Wayne Nance. I do not need to give that monster any more press than he already doesn't deserve.

The night he died

When the case of Wayne Nance, the serial killer, finally hit the news it was a bit of a shock to the town. We had ourselves our very own serial killer. He had snuck into the house of one of his victims but they had fought back, killing him in the process.

Both my sister and I thought back to our experiences, wondering if we had had a terrible brush with death or if the serial killer craze had just made us see ghosts where there weren't any.

Of all the people to clear it up, I didn't expect it to come from my mom. Ten years after I had spoken with my sister and heard her brush with uncertainty, I found myself with my mom and my sister at a family function. I had to ask my mom if she had anything strange happen while we lived up on the hill.

She, of course, said that my sister and I were idiots. She remembered both events. She thought we were being our typical high needs, hyperactive child selves. My mom asked me why I re-told her these stories and why I was asking. I told her that as I discussed it with my sister and started to put the signs in my life together that it well could have been our local serial killer, WN, as the man in the white pants.

That was one of the very few times in my life when I saw my mom's demeanor change from funny sarcastic to dead serious. You would have thought the story ended here, but no, leave it to my mom to add another weird coincidence that would be nothing short of another sign in my life.

You see, my mom had been on duty at the emergency room the night that Nance was wheeled in with a gunshot wound. She was there, about to operate on this man without knowing anything about who he was. He died on the operating table of the gunshot wound from a victim that he couldn't quite kill. My mom told us in no uncertain way that once they found out in the next few days who this person was, there was a collective sigh of relief from all attending that night that they did not help resurrect a monster.

I have wondered many times if I was on that list. Was I among those people that a serial killer had *almost* added to his list? Was my sister?

At this particular juncture in my life I could not have known either way, but I do know that I'm thankful to be alive. You see, the experiences that I have gone through have given me a gift much greater than simply survival. I can't just go from day to day anymore. They have made me aware of just how fragile life can be.

We might have a brush with death or worse once in a lifetime, or multiple times every day. But either way, I can now look at each day with a new awareness and gratitude for life that was granted to me by an unknown man who might have taken that life. It is a gift that I cherish, because it can disappear so easily.

My mom had seen it disappear, and was left to clean up what blood she could off the once white pants of a killer.

"Love is a Battlefield." —Pat Benatar

Chapter 2

A Sad Love Story

Somewhere out there, in a little municipal police office, lays a case file. It's in the solved homicide section, and contains recordings of three little traumatized boys trying to explain what they had seen and done that day.

We started out on a day like any other. Randy, Brion, and I were riding our bikes. About half a mile from town, we had set up a jump in a ditch where we would try to do tricks until one of us got hurt. This day, though, there was something weird on the way to the jump. In the front lawn of a little duplex, a big truck was parked at an angle towards the door. It wasn't super strange. "Probably just someone moving furniture" I said.

"The truck has a topper on the back," Randy said. "I don't think they're moving furniture."

"Fine, whatever," I said. The truck was still running. I just figured that whoever it was, was just lazy.

"Are those legs?" Randy said as he got closer.

Sticking out of the driver side door were a pair of legs. We stopped to see what was going on. Experience had taught us to keep our distance, but we got close enough to see the old man sitting on the ground.

"Hey, are you ok?" I asked him.

His eyes roamed around, occasionally stopping on us, but he didn't say anything. He looked disoriented or confused.

Finally, we left. We had tricks to do. And he was being weird. The ditch jump wasn't going to jump itself. And besides, it was light out and there were plenty of other people in the neighborhood. They could talk to him.

We were off to the jump. Once we got there, things went about like they usually do when you get a bunch of small kids trying to do tricks off a jump on bikes. We jumped for around ten minutes before Randy's little brother Brion fell on his ankle, twisting it badly. It turned out that it was only sprained, but for how loud he was screaming you would have thought it had snapped clean off. So we all got back on our bikes and started home.

Brion was screaming and whining the whole way, but to be frank, Randy and I were being assholes. We left him to make his way as best he could. When we got to the house, the truck was still there. So was the man, gazing off into space.

This time, when we asked him if he was ok, he managed to turn his head towards us, letting us see the dried blood that caked the back of his head.

As a group of prepubescent kids whose total experience with blood was self-inflicted stunts gone wrong, we did exactly what you would have expected us to do:

We shit ourselves.

Even Brion, sprained ankle and all, was on his bike and racing home faster than Lance Armstrong racing from a doping scandal. When we busted into Randy and Brion's parents, each of us started shouting about the blood as loud as we could. The chaos of our three voices managed to tell them what we saw, and the police got called.

We all went up to the house. The kids were told to stay in the car.

We should have listened.

The police officer started by talking to the old man and trying to help him. Something he said triggered Randy's dad and he ran to the back of the car. We got out of the car and followed him and for the first time noticed a hose running from the exhaust pipe of the car to the inside of the topper. When Randy's dad opened up the topper, it smelled like exhaust. Inside we saw something that made our blood run cold. It was a dead elderly woman, lying on a mattress.

When all of the police reports were done, we didn't hear anything more about it until a story ran in the news almost three months later.

It said that the old woman had been suffering from Alzheimer's and could barely recognize anyone. Her husband had been taking care of her while she deteriorated mentally, until he started to develop health problems as well. He had made the decision that it was time for them both to move on.

That day, he had backed his truck up to the door and wrestled the mattress up inside the back. He then maneuvered his wife up back there. He attached the hose to leak the exhaust into the back and planned for them to drift off to sleep together. With everything set up, he turned on the truck and slipped on the way back, hitting his head and knocking himself out. When we found him, he had woken, but was still disoriented. His wife, however, was already gone.

Instead of leaving with his wife, he was convicted of homicide. What started as love got twisted by the hands of fate. It was a truly sad love story.

I learned then that life isn't always fair and things don't always turn out right. But, we each have to live the life we've got.

"And I am not frightened of dying, any time will do, I don't mind." —Pink Floyd

Chapter 3

Death of Innocence

When I was a sophomore in high school, my parents got me a car. We went to the dealer and got a Hyundai Elantra, the only one they had on the lot. It was a beauty, all except for the color which happened to match just about perfectly to the purple color of Barney the dinosaur.

We called it the Purple Lamborghini.

This was back in my hometown again, and like I've said before, things were much more relaxed back in those days. Having a good time generally meant going to a party and parties meant drinking, regardless of your age. Our parents didn't necessarily approve, but they also didn't work very hard to stop us. There was a general consensus that as long as we didn't get into too much trouble, we could do what we wanted.

So one weekend we went up in the woods to have a party, like we usually did. It was going to be a good time. We didn't usually drive but I was feeling stupid, and we had heard some rumors that we could spend the night.

I stopped by my friend Andy's house to pick him up. We were off, slip sliding up the dirt road to get there. When we arrived, there were a lot of people there. This wasn't just a party. It was a full blown kegger.

There were kids from a few of the local high schools, and lots of alcohol. Andy and I were both fifteen at the time and life was our oyster... or at least his. I already had a girlfriend and was actually a little anxious to see her. Andy was working his teenage game and would get lucky that night. I was feeling impatient.

Between the alcohol and watching everyone else start to settle down with someone, my impatience was very quickly turning into anger. Andy said he was going to stay. I got drunkenly back into the Purple Lamborghini to drive to see my girlfriend.

It was getting pretty late. I had overwhelmed my fifteen-year-old physiology, and was struggling to work the controls of my car when I came upon a turn in the road. It was a tight curve on the way up when I was still sober. Now it was a death trap.

Luckily, no one was coming up the road. As I whipped around the turn, my tires started to squeal and slip on the road pushing my hazy brain into a drunken panic. I jerked the wheel to the right, trying hard to stop the motion of the car but really just overcorrecting.

When the wheels gained traction a second later, the whole car threw itself into the side of the mountain. The entire passenger side was smashed in, leaving me dazed as the car flipped over on itself.

When the dust settled, I was staring at the passenger seat where Andy sat on the way up to the party. If he had decided to come back down with me, he would have died. It would have been on my conscience.

I scrambled out the driver side window and wandered down towards the lights of a house three miles away. The couple there let me call my parents who came and picked me up.

Back at the party, a few of my friends were driving down the mountain. They had been smarter than I was and the driver of their car was sober. When they saw my car, panic set in. Even with the hood smashed in and on its head, they could recognize the shade of purple that so perfectly matched the magic dinosaur.

They stopped and started to search the car, looking for me. They could only find my jacket, left behind as I struggled to escape.

A police man pulled up to the wreck about the same time as my parents did, with me drunk and ashamed in the back seat. Through some strange act of grace, the officer was the father of one of my friends and about to retire.

When I had sobered up, he told me that he could have written me up. He could have brought down the full force of the law and destroyed my future, but he didn't. He knew what it would do. He knew that it would have blocked all my chances of going to college, and put a permanent mark on my record that I would never have gotten out from under. I knew that I was one argument from killing my best friend in a terrible accident.

He didn't write me up. I hadn't killed my friend.

I've found that sometimes, you have people looking out for you. Sometimes, you end up facing the full consequences of your own stupidity. There are two lessons to learn here.

First, don't drink and drive. It sounds trite. Just don't. A mere two years later, Andy would go up shooting in the mountains with some friends and start drinking. When they drove down in their Jeep Wrangler, he had his hand on the roll bar when the jeep tipped. He lost two fingers and it destroyed his dream of going into the Air Force. It could have been me.

Second, be grateful for the mercy of those who watch out for you, and forgive the mistakes that should condemn you. I didn't kill Andy, but my future could have turned out very similar to his.

That officer was what made the difference, not me.

"And the thunder rolls." —Garth Brooks

Chapter 4

Third Time's a Charm

Sometimes in your life, you get hit by lightning. It might be a physical lightning bolt or a metaphorical freak occurrence that shouldn't have happened to anyone. Those lightning bolts are often painful or shocking, but more than anything, they are rare. They are the phenomenon that define you.

So when I say that I've been struck by lightning three times, you might want to suspend your disbelief for just a few minutes while I try to explain the bizarre set of circumstances that have made up my experiences and why I can technically say that.

The first time I was struck was as a kid. I was only eight at the time. I was out in a field messing around with my friends Jim and Cory. We were young and just running around, playing. My home state is a pretty wild place. The storms there can sneak up on you if you're not careful. I still haven't met an eight-year-old who was careful.

So when a storm blew up on us, it wasn't the first time it had happened and it certainly wouldn't be the last. But what would make this one different was what happened as we raced across the open field with raindrops beginning to fall.

We ran like little kids do in the rain, yelling at being rained on but secretly thrilled at getting wet. At least until the lightning struck.

Static energy pricked at our prepubescent arm hair, standing all of them on end. We heard a loud boom that sent each of us reeling. And when I say reeling, I don't mean staggering because of the sound. When lightning hits, it sends a shockwave through the ground and air within ten yards with enough power to knock things out of whack. After that ten yards, it reduces to only an earsplitting sound wave. If you're caught in that shockwave, reeling might be too weak of a word to describe exactly what happens.

We were knocked on our butts, stunned, while wondering if we were still alive.

When we got home and had calmed down enough to check ourselves, we could still smell some of the burnt hair from our arms.

The second time I got struck was in college. My friend Glen and I were driving across the country to an internship in Washington D.C. with our state senator from the Blue Sky state. We had been driving for three days with almost no sleep; we also had been up late partying the night before, when we happened to find a branch of our college fraternity in the outskirts of Illinois. But we had to be in D.C. in forty-five hours, so we got up early and started driving, hangovers notwithstanding. We had gotten some weed earlier and decided, in our hungover state, that we might as well smoke a bowl or two to make the drive a little easier.

That afternoon, we started to notice some dark clouds piling up on the horizon. We continued driving, and it started to rain. At first, it was just a sprinkling. It very quickly picked up the pace. Before we knew it, the rain was like a sheet of water coming down from the heavens. When we could actually see out the windows, the clouds were blacker than coal and covering the whole sky ahead of us. Things didn't look good.

Ahead of us, some cars were pulling off the road but a few were still going ahead into the biggest, blackest storm clouds I had ever seen. We weren't sure whether we should keep going or not at this point. I had always heard the phrase "black as sin" and thought of it as nothing more than a religious metaphor. But at that moment, staring up into clouds that were darker than the sky at night, I wondered if I maybe I should have stopped by a confessional that morning.

Luckily (or maybe unluckily, I still haven't decided), Glen was there. I wasn't about to tell him that I was scared. So we did what any college kid would do. We smoked another bowl and forged ahead into the scariest storm of my life.

Five minutes later, I looked over at Glen in the driver's seat. His hands had a vice grip on the steering wheel and his eyes squinted to see through the gaps in the water left by the furiously flapping windshield wipers. In his eyes was a look that seemed to be a strange combination of utter terror, relaxation from the pot, and concentration on the dim red lights of the semi-truck ahead of us.

Rain pounded the car, and extreme wind threatened to push us off of the road. When I looked out the passenger side window, the rain wasn't so much falling as it was flying sideways.

In my nervousness, I had pulled out the little BIC lighter I had in my pocket and was playing with it. With the older lighters, you could remove the safety limiter on the flame size, turning them into a little blow torch. It was something to concentrate on so that I didn't have to see the windy, black hell we had mistakenly decided to drive straight into.

And then, without warning, the rain and the wind stopped.

In a strange silence, both Glen and I looked around dumbfounded at the small calm field that we had driven into. Lightning was striking all around us in a beautiful display of the raw power of nature.

Purple tinged light flashed repeatedly, lighting up the black sky that continued to hang ominously over our heads. The thunder was the only thing we could hear, and the silence became deafening.

I reached over and turned on the radio, hoping to get some idea as to what we were driving through. After some small talk, we heard a loud, obnoxious sound that blared through the car.

"BRRRRRRRRRRRRRK! BRRRRRRRRRRRRRK! BR-RRRRRRRRRRRRK! This is the emergency broadcast system. The National Weather Service has announced a tornado warning. A tornado has been sighted near Lake Erie, mile marker 115."

Glen and I knew we were close to that area, but we didn't know how close until we saw the next sign that read the three numbers that we both least wanted to see: 115. We continued on the road. Glen was laser focused on the truck in front of us. I was taking turns playing with the lighter and frantically looking around to see if I could see the tornado that could throw our car with us in it.

I would learn later that we had driven through an F4 tornado supercell. The actual tornado was powerful enough to throw cars and tear down houses. Large missiles were generated, and all of the stunning lightning we were seeing was part of the supercell.

Finally, we broke out of the center of the cell and the rain and wind pounded into us again. Rain began to slam into the side of our car combatting the inadequate windshield wipers that had remained on, forgotten through the eye of the storm. I reached down to flick on the little BIC lighter in my hand when everything went white. My brain registered the light and simultaneously told me that a shotgun had gone off in the car, right next to my head.

When my vision cleared, almost ten seconds later, we were still driving behind the semi-truck. Glen was frantically glancing between the truck lights and the lighter in my hands. Anger became confusion when he saw the still-intact lighter.

"I thought the lighter had exploded," he yelled into my still ringing ears. I nodded silently as the smell of burnt hair crept into my nose.

Ten miles later, the rain let up and we saw the clouds above us begin to lighten up. Glen pulled off the road and we shakily got out of the car. Smoke was rising from the hood of the car, starting at a point where the paint was slightly discolored. Behind us the car that had been following our lights had pulled off behind us. The driver got out of the car with a look of shock on his face.

"Are you guys alright?" he asked incredulously.

"Yeah," I said. "I think so."

"I just watched lightning hit your car," he said, still trying to take it in. "How did you not jerk the wheel and fly off the road?" he asked.

I glanced down at the bowl sitting in the car with amazement.

"I don't know," Glen said. "I just let go of the wheel for a sec and then grabbed it again."

We got back into our cars and kept driving. I couldn't help but stare at that pipe and wonder at it all. I had been struck by lightning once before and walked away with nothing more than a few bruises from falling down. This time, I had even less to show.

There were so many poor choices that we had made. Between being hungover, high, exhausted, and in the middle of a tornado supercell we should have been in trouble six different ways without getting hit by the lightning. That it all worked together to keep us alive was a coincidence of the very highest order.

If we hadn't been driving straight through, we wouldn't have happened upon the fraternity and gotten drunk the night before. Without them, we wouldn't have been hungover leading to the weed to soften the ride. When we drove into that storm, it was stupid. But when lightning struck, Glen's reflexes were slow and he didn't jerk the wheel. He didn't flinch. We kept driving instead of crashing on the way to D.C.

The first-time lightning struck, I was a kid, and it was startling. Shocking even.

The second time, we were asking for something to go wrong in the most spectacular of ways.

But the third bolt was one of those metaphorical ones where everything falls just perfectly, saving us from ourselves.

I still can't explain exactly why we walked away from that lightning bolt. It doesn't make sense. At the very least, we should have ended up on the side of the road with something damaged. I'm not sure whether or not this was something divine saving my life or just a well-timed bit of weed. But either way, I'm grateful.

Chance J.J. Edric

"Once upon a time in a land far away..." —Missio

Chapter 5

Hang 'em High

This is somewhat a departure from the crux of most of my stories. But it fits in its own way. Also, it is just too fucking good to pass up. Furthermore, it's a dedication to Hambone: one hell of a southern gentlemen that graced my life through marriage to my older sister. Hambone is a legend in so many ways. Sadly, Hambone and his good friend Billy Bob have left this plane of existence and are roping the wind in the beyond. With the blessing from Hambone's son, here are how parts of this beautiful world can still beat to their own drum.

I met Hambone in my junior year of college, right about the time my wife and I started doing the good ol' college hustle. My wife had the pleasure of his acquaintance the entire ride that we had with him on this earth. And what a ride it was.

Hambone was from the bowels of America. Well, the Texas / Louisiana bowels. A nice little town by the name of Mount Pleasant. Sounds lovely, right? This was about as backwoods as it got in Texas. Some might argue the panhandle has that wrapped up but the stories Hambone would tell us gave me the impression that Mount Pleasant took that title.

Hambone was a very tall, very lanky fellow. My sister met him at some country bar on the fringe of our hometown. There was something about his grace and old school gentlemanly demeanor that took her back. That said, you could barely understand this fellow. His southern drawl was so thick with a Texan accent that it was only about every third word that you could make out. He also had this other crazy north Louisiana dialect which made a perfect storm for communication issues and innocent comedy.

This southern gentleman was genuinely as kind as they come and had manners for days which led him to quickly become a beloved member of our family. Everyone loved his humor and storytelling which allowed us to know him a little more intimately. Ham also had more than a few dark secrets. His darkest was that he lived life hard and was hard on his body with his past accomplishments and current affairs. He could drink anyone under the table. Sometimes, Ham would get an edge of anger with a hard night of beers and booze. Nothing terrible mind you, just not the normal southern gentlemen we knew from being new to the family.

The one story he told us, in his slightly altered state, was interpreted by my sister and it was a real humdinger. With my sister's and his remaining son's permission, I will gladly recant the oral history he gave us all that long-ago December night.

I told you where Ham was from. Also, please remember that the story he told us happened nearly 30 years ago. Moonshine and horses are just a way of life in an idyllic little town. And the convergence of Louisiana backwoods and North Texas pride still hover in the air.

Hambone had a good drink buzz going on that cold December night in Missoula. The majority of the family was together that night. It was one of those nights perfect for getting together and celebrating life. It was with that nice buzz and happiness vibe that he decided to tell everyone about the night he hung a man. We all stopped what we were doing. We looked at my sister for some sort of affirmation and possible translation in case we just heard him wrong. My sister only nodded and told us that she already knew this story to be true as Hambone's family had told her all about it when she was last back in Mount Pleasant. It's all true.

This was back in the day when Ham was well into his prime and winning plenty of Buckles and Horse Saddles. Ham had gone to the Vegas National Rodeo twelve separate times. At one time, he ranked 15th in the nation. He was as good as good could be back in the heyday. He was damn proud of those accomplishments. A hard worker all the way around.

His best friend, Billy Bob? Well, he was just as accomplished. Just, in different avenues of life's little opportunities. Billy Bob had ran afoul of the law more than a few times in his storied, unfortunately too short, life. Billy Bob was an incredible friend though. Loyal as blood. Thick as family. Ham and Billy Bob were never very far from each other. Sometimes for good, sometimes for bad.

Jerry Starkwell was an outsider in all of this. He was known around the small town of Mount Pleasant, he just didn't play to society's standards. He spent most of his adult life in and out of jail for burglary and other petty crimes. Of course, he was always around the same few dive bars. Hambone and Billy Bob would frequently run into Jerry. Jerry would listen to their tales of comradery and to Hambone recant his various Rodeo wins.

One random day when Hambone came home from a two week stay in Las Vegas, he noticed that his front door was ajar. Mad at himself for leaving his door unlocked, Hambone went in with reckless abandon. Right away it hit him. As he surveyed the clutter and upturned furniture in his house, he only had two thoughts: his gun safe and his prized contest saddles. A quick walk to his room gave him a sweet sigh of relief. His huge safe was still locked. He had quickly looked inside and yes, everything was there. He picked up his Colt 45 and slowly walked to the garage where he kept his other valuables. His heart sank when he opened the doors. His three prized championship saddles that he had won were gone from their hanging spots. And while they were worth a good chunk of money, it was the lost physical connection to amazing memories that crushed him that day. He was steaming mad at his point. The local police were sympathetic to Ham when they searched the house, but there was little they could do. A few other things were taken, although not nearly as much of a loss as those three saddles. Some broken things had to be trashed. The cops would ask and look around, but with the way the folk worked around these parts they were afraid to talk to the law. There were multiple opportunities to make money around this area. Hell, Moonshining was still a thing and a very profitable business. So it was with a heavy heart that Hambone accepted that he may never see those saddles again.

Billy Bob came back to town a week later. He had been out hunting and chasing some of those other opportunities. When he and Ham got together to catch up and drink some 'shine, it was then that Billy Bob heard about the robbery. He assured Ham he would use every single one of his resources to help track down whoever did this. And like a true and loyal friend, Billy Bob actually came through.

As it turned out, one of Billy Bob's clients a few counties over just happened to turn down a random guy who was trying to pawn three horse saddles. All three were national prize saddles, he was sure of it. The other good news was that the pawn shop owner got this guy's name: Jerry Starkwell. No sooner had Billy Bob said his name than Hambone was flying out the door towards his truck. Billy Bob, like the loyal friend he was, knew that this had to be fixed and he had no choice but to back up his best friend. Out the door he flew, watching Ham pick up some supplies on the way out the door and throw them into the back of the truck.

They knew exactly where Jerry resided. They also knew his regular haunts. Lo and behold he was not at home. The place was dark. They also struck out at the next three stops as they barreled through town. It was one of the last dive bars that they visited where they found their prize. Jerry was sitting in the back yelling some nonsense to one of the other regulars in the bars. Jerry didn't see Ham or Billy Bob coming. Hambone picked him up by the neck and the look on Jerry's face told both men everything. Billy Bob looked around the bar and knowingly at the bartender and said very calmly that this establishment was not the place to extract any information on the location of Hambone's stolen property. Ham thought through his rage and quickly agreed. They dragged poor Jerry Starkwell out of the door past an onslaught of onlookers, who just stared at all men with understanding eyes. Not a single patron moved to stop any of it. They knew each man involved and this was a county of residents who knew they dispensed their own law in these parts.

In the truck, both men were very quiet. Hambone finally opened up after Jerry's third or fourth plea to be let go. Hambone asked a very simple question. He wanted to know where his prized saddles were. When Jerry vehemently denied any knowledge of said stolen items, Billy Bob brought up the pawn shop owner's name where he tried to sell them. His face now ashen white, Jerry said he still had them back at his house. He was unable to unload them.

That's when the truck came to a screeching halt over the old bridge at Lake Monticello. They dragged Jerry out of the truck, gave him a few love taps for good measure, then Hambone retrieved one of the items he had brought with him. A large gauge rope. Hambone tied up a knot he knew all too well from his years of roping. Jerry was pleading and struggling to no avail. Hambone swiftly threw the open knot around Jerry's neck. Without any warning he yanked Jerry from Billy Bob's arms and threw him over the side of the bridge. Hambone and Billy Bob held on to the other end of the rope. For that reason alone Jerry's neck did not immediately snap. While the knot tightened, he was heavy enough that he dragged both Ham and Billy Bob a few feet. There Jerry swung, his feet dangling into nothingness and over a thirty-yard drop to the lake below. This time Jerry had gone too far.

Billy Bob sat silently next to Hambone as they both gripped the rope that was struggling less and less. It was about that time that a sigh of relief went through his lips. Hambone told him to pull Jerry up; he had changed his mind about something. The rope had stopped all movement on the other side at this point. The two men pulled up the limp body of Jerry Starkwell. Surprisingly, as they let his body slam back down on the bridge, Jerry started to gasp for air. Hambone took his rope from around Jerry's neck and threw him in the back of the truck. He let Jerry know that they were going to retrieve his property and then discuss this further. They drove in long silence to Jerry's house. Sure enough, the saddles were in his guest room. Bobby Joe and Hambone grabbed the saddles and gave Jerry the ultimatum that he was to clear out of town by the morning or they would come back and finish the job. It was time for Jerry to call a different town his home. They stormed out and left Jerry to his own thoughts and a blistering rope burn.

You might think that would be the end of it. But there was one more life lesson Jerry Starkwell would have to endure that night.

On the side of the law, Jerry Starkwell did the right thing. About an hour after Hambone and Billy Bob left him, he got enough courage to head to the local Sheriff's office. He stormed in on the Sheriff and a couple of his deputies playing a game of poker. It was a small town and a lot of the justice was dealt with locally, so the police were very surprised to see a well-known face walk through the door, one that they knew all too well. So well they told Jerry that it was weird to see him come through the front door instead of the back door.

When the laughter subsided, Jerry began to rant angrily about his last few hours. Of course, the police were listening to this new story with interest. It was a supposed attempted homicide; it was their duty. As Jerry finished the story, the Sheriff sat for a moment before he asked him only one question:

"Well. Why in the world would Hambone and Billy Bob do such a thing? Surely there was a reason?"

Jerry Starkwell sunk his head and shuffled his feet but eventually answered the Sheriff. He told him bluntly that he stole Hambone's three championship saddles and tried to hawk them for drug and booze money.

"Well then. I suppose it's time for you vacate the town. Oh, and stop stealing will ya? Liable to get killed over that someday."

The Sheriff turned around and resumed his game with the other deputies. Jerry slinked out the front door without a single glance back.

Never purposefully steal a person's pride. Not only is it rude, it's theirs. They are right any way you want to put it. It's theirs.

And for God sake, if you are stupid enough to actually steal their pride, don't be an idiot and try to sell it. That's just asking for bad karma.

"We are spirits in the material world." —The Police

Chapter 6

Something Out of the Ordinary

I have spent many years looking for signs: signs in the heavens, signs of hell, signs someone cared about me and my life. I can't say that I ever found anything convincing. There was never anything concrete. I know that there are a lot of people out there looking to believe in something bigger, grander, or more powerful than themselves, and I don't blame them for it. I spent years looking for it myself. I get it. I just didn't find anything.

To be clear, if you're a Christian, Jew, Muslim, or Buddhist, I don't care. I'm not disputing what you believe. Everyone can believe what they want. In fact, that's one of the few things I *have* come to really know. There's just not enough proof to say anything, one way or the other.

And as for all those signs? You don't find them. They tend to find you.

During a Midwestern winter storm on December 23, we found ourselves on the highway. The roads were barren with the exception of a few iced-over cars inching their way along to wherever they were going to spend the holidays. Traffic had slowed to a crawl, with people not willing to jeopardize their celebrations with excessive speed.

No one except for us, that was. And that was because it was time.

My wife was due, and our son was ready to come into the world. The last nine months had been a wonderland of my wife's vomit, pain, and anger that was all culminating in this one moment in the next hour: or so we thought. We didn't know it at the time, but our son was coming into the world with his defiant devil-may-care attitude that would wreak havoc on his mother, his father, and even his own body.

Seventeen long hours later, his screaming little head saw the light for the first time, followed by the rest of his enraged body, punching and kicking with all his might. His face was so red that it started turning purple as his mouth let out an enraged cry. After nine months of comfort, this was nothing short of a traumatic experience, and he did not appreciate it at all.

As if trying to get back at us, he was hard on us all from the start. First, the doctors took him to the NICU for tests, worrying that his breathing might not be right. It turned out to be fine, but he wasn't done yet.

Have you ever heard of a baby with colic? It's one thing to hear about a fussy baby, but another thing altogether to live with one. It means that instead of just having to get up every few hours to feed the crying baby, he will also cry when he is not hungry. And cry whether he needs to be changed or doesn't. He'll cry all the time. In fact, the way you diagnose colic is to watch whether he has crying fits longer than three *hours*, three days a week, for longer than three weeks. That is a lot of crying. Again, it's one thing to hear about it, and another to experience all the piss and vinegar that his tiny little body could hold.

And we loved him for it.

Life's little wonderful packages are amazing. The little beings that come into our lives bring emotions that are completely new and wonderful. And they are even more powerful when a few of those little packages didn't quite make it.

Imagine that life has made you the most amazing promise you can think of. It makes you giddy and nervous just to think about it. You get all excited, waiting for it to arrive when suddenly you get the news that it isn't.

It was in those moments that I wanted to see the signs. I wanted reasons. I wanted to know *why* it had to happen. And there were no answers to be had. All I could think about was how that gift of life had been taken from us. I would never know what abilities or talents they might have had. I would never get to see whose nose they had or whose eyes. And I wanted to know why.

Maybe I was ignoring the signs. Maybe I just didn't want to see them then. It was hard to believe in anything god-like in the wake of tragedy. But with a little time, and a few signs that we couldn't ignore, I came to believe that there *is* something out there. Some other force working on something, even if we don't get what's going on all the time. It's not my job to sell you on it, but I promise you that every single story in this book is the truth.

It started when my son was conceived. When we first moved into our house, three years before, it was almost brand-new. It had been built only eight years before we got there. There wasn't even enough time for anything creepy to happen to it yet. We were in a typical suburban neighborhood on the right side of town and even had a rising NFL star living across the street. We didn't live next to any creepy old buildings or on the remains of a Native American burial ground but we started to see little things happening.

First my wife saw them, and then I started to notice them too. Tiny things that couldn't really be explained. A book flew off the shelf and landed fifteen feet away. At night, we would hear footsteps in the attic above us. But for whatever reason, we weren't scared. It wasn't the kind of haunting that you usually hear about in the movies. The book wasn't trying to hit someone. And the footsteps? They sounded like two little children playing. With my son on the way, and tragedy in our past, the little sounds and signs actually ended up being comforting. Unnerving at the time they happened, for sure, but not in a warning-written-on-the-wall-in-blood sort of way. We never felt like we were in any danger, and there was never any fear.

The day that my son finally came into the world, everything was amazing. My wife and I were exhausted, although I'll admit that she did most of the work. I went and got her a gift to remember the day. Our son meant the world to us, and I wanted her to have a way to always remember the day he came into our lives.

It was a simple twist-tie styled bracelet with a little duck charm from Tiffany's. On the back of the charm it had our son's name and birthday, etched in the metal like it was etched in my mind. I wasn't trying to break the bank, and the bracelet wasn't super expensive. It was a perfect little reminder of a wonderful day.

Life went on, and between changing diapers and sleepless nights, we did too. My wife wore that little bracelet all the time, and we loved our little boy like only new parents can.

Then one day, I got home and found my wife with a look that instantly put me on edge.

"What happened to our son?" I asked, concerned. Force of habit told me that he was the one that I needed to worry about, and when I walked in the door to see her frantically pacing around the room, my thoughts immediately jumped to him.

"Nothing," she said, unconvincingly. "I mean he's fine."

With my first priority taken care of, I felt like I could calm down a little bit before asking her, "So what happened?"

"I'm just not sure where I left my bracelet," she finally admitted. "I misplaced it somewhere. Between dropping him off at daycare, getting coffee, and teaching all day, it disappeared."

Of all the things that could have gone wrong, this one seemed manageable. "That's okay. No big deal. Let's just retrace your steps and figure out where you put it."

So we did. We started in the obvious places: the car, the school, and the coffee shop. But when it didn't show up, we started looking a little harder. We tore the car apart and then started going through our house room by room, hoping that it would turn up. But we couldn't find it. Eventually, we resigned ourselves to the idea that maybe it would just show up.

But a month later, it still hadn't. It started to seem less like she had misplaced it somewhere where we could get it back. Maybe it had fallen off outside and been picked up by someone else. Maybe it was sitting in someone else's home, found on the sidewalk.

A year later, it was obvious that the bracelet was gone. I knew what it meant to her, and I knew that I was going to get her a new one. It was just that kind of gift.

Two years later, life was moving on, as it does, and I had yet to actually buy the bracelet. I had looked at Tiffany's and found one that was close, but it was going to run me another eight hundred dollars. I was still shopping around, seeing if I could find something less expensive. After all, this one was close, but the charm was a little different and it wasn't *exactly* the same. Maybe I could find something close to it but for a little cheaper?

I was still in that shopping-around phase, slowly checking places out in the time gaps between normal life, when something strange happened.

I was going to listen to my favorite band of all time: Pearl Jam. I really should have known something would come up. Something always comes up when I go to Pearl Jam concerts. This one was back home where I grew up, and was that much more special. The band had returned to my hometown and I would see a sold-out show with some great friends. We were tailgating and partying, and the weather was spectacular. It was one of those days where you almost wish you could just stop time and enjoy it forever.

We were waiting to go in when I got the call from my wife. She and my son had stayed at home while I went to the concert. She was an angel for staying with him, and I wasn't about to ignore the call. But as soon as I picked up the phone, I could tell that something was wrong. Her voice was panicked. No, that is an understatement. To this day, I have never heard the concern so heavy in her voice.

"What happened to our son?" I asked, instantly sober. She sounded distracted.

"What? Oh, nothing. He slept two and a half hours straight, so that's good," she said, obviously not what was worrying her.

"Awesome!" I said, "New record, right?"

"Yeah, but that's not it."

"What's wrong then?" I asked, wondering what could be more wrong than our son.

"I found the bracelet."

I was instantly excited. I was going to see Pearl Jam *and* save eight hundred dollars?

"That's awesome!" I said.

"No," she said, "It's *how* I found it."

Now before I tell you the story, we need to get one thing straight. Ava? She's not a liar. She doesn't even fib. She's so straight that it can be annoying. Where other people tell white lies to make you feel better when you got a botched haircut, she'll just call it like it is. She even has a cameo guest chapter within this book where you read her straight shooter sensibility. It's just a part of her DNA. So when I heard this story over the phone, it did more than just send chills up my spine. It really got me thinking.

It was a totally normal day. She got up and played with our son during the morning. She fed him and rocked him to get the air bubbles out. Then she started cleaning the house like she normally did. Around noon he started to get fussy like he normally did and she finished vacuuming before putting him down. He's a pretty light sleeper so she was really careful to close the door and tip toe out. They were the only two in the house and now that she had some peace and quiet, she decided to get in a quick nap herself.

Two and a half hours later she woke up to his shrill little cries echoing from the baby monitor by her side. It had become our normal alarm clock these days and she lifted herself off of the couch to go and get him. She walked up the stairs, opened the door, and stopped.

Sitting there in the middle of the floor, laid out in a *perfect little vertical line*, was the bracelet.

Her mind raced to the different possibilities.

Maybe it was in the vacuum and it just got spit out? Well, the vacuum had been bought new within the past few months.

Was it hidden in the furniture? Not possible. The rocking chair, crib, and dresser had each been taken apart and cleaned in the past two years, specifically when looking for that bracelet.

In fact, we had torn our whole damn house apart looking for that bracelet and our son's room was no exception. It simply wasn't there; and then it was, like it had been waiting to be seen and picked up from the day it disappeared.

"Leave," I said, instantly. "Get a bag together and go to a hotel." I was suddenly acutely aware of each of the 2000 miles that separated us and just how unable I was to help her in that moment. "I'll be home tomorrow afternoon, and we can work this all out then."

She was still in shock and afraid of what might have happened, but she murmured in agreement and hung up. A few hours later, I got a text saying that she was going to stay. I was more than a little nervous, but I knew that she would do what she felt was best.

The next day I found her at home, looking remarkably refreshed. The lesson she taught me was a powerful one.

She said that she went into that room and simply said, "Thank you for returning this precious piece of jewelry to me. It is very important to me, and I am incredibly grateful." She told me that she had finally recognized just how important the little things can really be. When she had finished speaking to the empty room, our son laughed at something in the corner. What was more, for the first time in his life he slept through the entire night, and let my wife do the same.

I learned that those little things, the ones that don't seem like a big deal at the time, can make a big difference. But more than that I learned that our lives have the meaning that *we* give them. *Each of us* has these little moments in our lives. Moments that change us and impact us. What changes us most of all is what we learn in those moments. We each become better or worse because of how we see and interpret those little moments, those little signs.

When that bracelet disappeared, we could have gotten depressed. When it showed up we could have totally freaked out. In fact, maybe we did a little bit of both. But we also chose to find a deeper meaning and gratitude in each. And I think we are much better for it.

This book wasn't meant to be a Jack London classic. Although a boy can dream. Which is the point of it all; I was hoping to inspire a few people and maybe change a few opinions along the way. Since this is my second edition of this book, I can happily report that I got those hopes and then a whole lot more.

Hopefully, you can forgive me a little on the formatting or any grammatical errors you may find. I had help but even the best help can miss common errors. And that gets back to the purpose of this book as well: we *all* make errors.

This book was meant to be something less and yet something more. It's meant to show those little moments that have made me who I am, and those little moments that you, *yes you*, have and will continue to have throughout life. You just need to pay attention. Or listen to others that have been there. Trust me. As you read these coming chapters of my crazy life you will see, or hopefully even remember, your own brushes with the things we do not see daily.

I hope to provoke the hell out of your memory all the while giving you a little entertainment in the process.

Cheers.

"I fell into a burning ring of fire, I went down, down, down." —Johnny Cash

Chapter 7

Poopy Pants Bandit

George had a look of horror plastered on his face, but the rest of us could only laugh. In a sudden jerking motion, he had thrown his suitcase down on the ground and was fighting to get it open, hoping for his own sake that all of the pants in it were his.

We were all on our way out of town, saying goodbye after a crazy weekend. The news story we just heard had just about sent us to the floor with laughter. It was too much for us. Well, all of us but George, that is.

You see, it had all started a few days before when we all arrived for our Alma Mater's homecoming football game. We had all graduated long since, but the games were a great time to get back together and root for the home team (go Griz!). We all met up the day before the game and did what we usually do: we celebrated.

We celebrated at one of the local bars where we had gone drinking when we were much younger, and where Georgy had worked back in college. Now if you're going to understand how we party, you've got to understand that we grew up together in a time that was way different from today.

Growing up back then was a much more relaxed time. Today, parents get in trouble for leaving their kids at home while they go grocery shopping to feed them. Back then, anything was allowed as long as you didn't break anything too big. We could generally do what we wanted. And in a town like ours that usually meant drinking, especially in college. We learned the best ways to drink for every occasion: there was the polite stuff you did with the girls at the bar and then there was the kind of drinking you did with your friends to prep for a big game.

That night, we were drinking like we hadn't seen each other for years. That wasn't quite true, but between having a good time and the game the next day, we were all getting pretty plastered. And George got the worst of it.

It was probably a good thing that George worked in the bar and knew the owner. At some point in the night, he had finally passed his limit. He staggered into the bathroom and locked the door. From outside we could hear him making out with the toilet and then as near as we could tell, he passed out.

I'm not usually the person who leaves a friend behind when he's passed out, but George was about as close as he was going to get to home. We felt comfortable enough with him being there. When he was out, we each finally said our goodbyes and got taxis home.

The next morning was the big game. Each of us woke up to that feeling like every light is trying to bore a hole through your head. We were hungover. But, we knew that the big game was that day so we did what any normal person would do to get ready for it: we started drinking again.

We were at the tailgate party when we heard George's story of the night before. He told us he had gotten a cab at some point during the night and made his way back home. When he woke in the morning, his pants were soaked.

We sniggered like little boys, thinking we knew exactly what happened.

But no, he said, it wasn't that. He pulled them off and smelled them and it definitely wasn't urine. And it wasn't like it was just that spot either; his pants were soaked from the legs to the waist. He admitted that he was blackout drunk, but he knew that he hadn't pissed himself.

We made the jokes anyway. What are friends for, right?

Eventually we got in and went to the game. Hometown team won. Usual. Suck it Kitty Kat fans! It was a good game. But the part of the story that remains forever in my memory was what happened when all of us got together to say goodbye. That night on the news there was the strangest story...

A man had reported a break in and theft to the police. Someone had broken into his house the night before and stolen a pair of pants and the keys to his car that were in them. Whoever it was had driven his car into the river. But that wasn't even the best part. The strangest thing was what the thief had left behind.

He left a pair of pants that had been pooped in.

Now let's get clear here. They were not a pair of pants with a little brown stain, or with skid marks in them. There were mushed up logs.

As best the police could tell, the thief broke in *after shitting himself* and stolen a new pair of pants. In their pocket, he just happened to find a set of keys and decided to go for a joyride until the river stopped him.

When we had told the story to George, he was horrified. He knew that he had been blackout drunk, but this was crazy. Each time he pulled out a pair of pants from his suitcase he held it up, examining it thoroughly as if trying to remember where exactly he had bought it.

Finally he turned to us and said, with no small sense of relief, "It wasn't me. They're all mine."

From then on, we couldn't help ourselves. The legend of the poopy pants bandit would haunt poor Georgy for the rest of his life. Of course he was sure that it wasn't him, and we all said that we believed him.

But we never did figure out what had soaked his pants.

"Party like it's 1999." —Prince

Chapter 8

Side Quests for Everyone

Regardless of year. Regardless of material goods or services rendered. What is the best thing you've ever spent $20 on? What is the best thing you've ever done for $20? Did you get a great meal? Did you spend it on your soul? Maybe it was a cheap date that turned out really well?

Think about it before you move on to reading the below short story. I love to ask thought provoking questions. It tends to feed the soul and help you think about those fantastic moments we've all experienced, but sadly forgotten.

I try to ask this question to every random person I encounter. While the responses vary, there definitely is a trend with each sex and the age of said person answering.

Sadly, the response I get from men tends to always involve some sort of sexual gratification. Whether it was an outright act of sex, or a date that was easy and inexpensive that led to a night of love. Now, I am not condemning anyone in this book or making any judgements. I refuse to do so. I think that every person's answer is their own and is absolutely correct. It is interesting that our stereotypes of each sex are almost always spot on. Men are visual and physical beings. Always will be.

Now women. Well, they fit the stereotype as well. I think I might have only heard a couple answers related to sex. That said, I always get a very long, thought out, and structured answer. It is always attached to an emotion. An object that was inexpensive that carried some sort of lifelong meaning. A doll they got from a father who soon passed or went away. A trip to somewhere they experienced some sort of euphoria.

I only point these out to jar your short or long-term memory of something special in your life that did not cost a ton of money, but made a huge impact on your soul, character, or way of looking at the world around you. Always looking for those signs.

I've got a story for you about a time I spent $20 and got the experience of a lifetime.

My friend (Bob) and I were in D.C. on business and decided to spend a free day off in Philadelphia. The day was good, but for the most part it was unremarkable. One of our friends was working in town and we got to spend a little time with him. That night though, something bizarre happened.

We were walking through a suburb in the cool night air when we saw a small venue with a line wrapped around the block. We were a little confused as to what could be happening to attract that kind of crowd in a small little place like this.

It was called the Pyramid, and could fit maybe a hundred people inside. As we asked around, up and down the line, no one could tell us what was going on. All that they knew was that it was big. I even talked to the bouncer who just told us that there was a $19.99 cover charge to get in.

$19.99 just to get into a crowded bar? It seemed a little steep for a college kid. I wasn't even sure what was going on. For all I knew, it could be one of those gags where some guy starts staring at the ceiling in the mall to see how many people he can get to stand and stare with him.

Bob and I decided we didn't really have anywhere better to be, and might as well see what was going on. We stood in line for a long time. I remember pulling out that twenty-dollar bill with Andrew Jackson's face on it and wondering whether or not it would actually be worth it in the end.

When we did finally get to the front of the line, we each got our penny back and filed into the room. It was dark and intimate. We filled in past a fire code sign that said the maximum capacity was around a hundred and fifty people. We must have been close to that inside.

There was one other thing about this place that you couldn't help but notice: everything was in purple. There were curtains and lights and the whole deal, all in that particular shade of purple that could only mean one thing.

Sure enough, at 1:30 AM, guess who walks in? None other than the purple one. Prince.

Apparently, this was a relatively normal occurrence for Prince. He would play a big show in a bigger town and then go to a small dive, unadvertised, later to do an after party. I'm not sure if it was his way of giving back, or just winding down after a big concert. They were never announced and only really found through rumors or (in our case) stupid luck.

For the next three and a half hours, we sat entranced as we listened to Prince play and sing whatever he wanted. The only hit I can remember him playing was a mixed-up version of *When Doves Cry*, but none of us even cared. It was a beautiful, intimate, and almost surreal experience. By the time we left, a little after 4:00 AM, we would only agree that we were $20 poorer and one amazing experience richer.

Now what do you have? I guarantee you have one. Everyone does.

"When it hasn't been your day, your week, your month, or even your year." —The Rembrandts

Chapter 9

Ross. From Friends

This story is a little bit different from some of the others in this book. It's not about me. In fact, I'm just the friend on the periphery for this one. But the story is memorable, tragic, and worth repeating. The lesson is worth learning. So before I start this one off, you need to know the hero of the story: Chris.

Chris is a spectacular guy. He's really smart when it comes to school, and always got good grades. He was the type of guy that you looked at and just thought, 'he has his stuff together.' But when you get to know him, he's one of those guys who can't tie his shoes without messing it up. Book smart but street dumb. Today, you'd probably even think he's cute if men are your thing. He's six foot flat and 185 lbs. lean. All muscle and bulk that he's kept up from his days in the Marines.

There's just one thing you really need to know about Chris. He's terrible with women. They are his Achilles heel.

Now when I say that, I don't mean that he mistreats them, or that he's abusive. He's just horrible at picking them. The ones he decides to stay with end up following a pattern that he just can't quite seem to escape.

When Chris was in high school, he was dating this girl. They were typical high school sweethearts, but it wasn't exactly what you'd call a functional adult relationship. In fact, it had more in common with sitcoms than with a healthy marriage. Think just about every relationship that Ross got into on *Friends*. It was drama, followed by a fight, followed by getting back together, even when everyone around them was groaning.

So when they decided to get married after high school, the two of them were the only ones who were really on board with it. Their families thought it was a bad idea. So did all of his friends. We knew he liked her. But sometimes that's just not enough.

And then there was the moment in 21 Palms while he was in the Marines. They hadn't gotten married yet, but he kissed some girl in a bar. Kind of cheating, but nothing more ever happened. That should have been the end of it. Except that he held on to it.

They finally got married and life seemed wonderful. Actually, that might be a bit of an exaggeration. They moved out to Hawaii for his work and I really didn't hear much from them. I assume that things went well at least for a little bit. I also suspect that their relationship went about like it always had in high school: on and off in cycles until you felt like you should have gotten off the rollercoaster two twists ago.

Two years later, I finally got the call from Chris. He told me about how they had a serious fight and in the middle of it, he brought up the kiss. I don't know if it was out of spite or drunken stupidity, but the results were the same. Chris got divorced.

A few years later, I heard from him again. This time, Chris was in New Mexico. He was working for AT&T and dealing with their electronics. Why do I get the call? Because he's seeing someone again.

This new girl and he have been dating for a while, and he's just about ready to pop the question. I admit that I tried to play the good friend and asked him all of the right questions. You know, the ones like, how did you meet? What's she like? Is she *the one*?

Immediately, his answers started to sound both familiar and alarming.

They had dated and then broken up *four times* by this point. I think he took the fact that they had gotten back together four times as a good sign. I wasn't so sure. And then there was the fact that they had almost nothing in common. When I asked him what they liked to do together, I honestly wasn't trying to stump him. I learned she ate everything gluten free and he loved any food you put in front of him.

In fact, about the only thing they had in common was that they both wanted to get married. I'm not sure if it was to each other that they wanted to be married, or to just be married to someone. Either way, the wedding was planned and she had just gotten pregnant.

Wonderful, I thought. Either they'll have something new to fight about, or something to inspire them to stay together. What a shame they weren't even the slightest bit compatible as human beings.

I watched Chris walk down the aisle with his second wife and wondered what was going to happen. Little did I know that they had already decided that it wasn't going to work. A few days before the wedding, she revealed that the baby might not be his. When I first heard, I assumed that it came from one of the times they had broken up but Chris was quick to correct me. No, she had cheated on him at a Christmas party not long before, "messing around" with another guy.

I was dumbfounded. "Why did you go through with the wedding then?" I asked.

"Simple. We had already spent so much money on the wedding and the honeymoon that it seemed a waste to not go through with it."

I wasn't sure if that second wedding was a total sham, or just another stupid choice made for women he didn't really love. I suspect the latter.

Not long after, they did the paternity test and found out that Chris wasn't actually the father.

The news should have been devastating. It should have called for a somber mood. So what did Chris do? In true Maury style, he went to Las Vegas to have a "Not My Baby" party. After all, he didn't have any ties to the child, and wouldn't have to pay child support.

They weren't even divorced yet.

That first day in Las Vegas, Chris and some of his friends met a few nineteen-year-old girls from Canada. Being a well-built attractive man had its perks, and Chris went after one of them with a passion. When they woke up in the same bed the next morning, Chris was in love.

He came home from Las Vegas and told us that he had finally found her. He had found the one. It was hard to watch at this point. We met her, but it was hard to like the girl. It wasn't for any fault in her. She was plenty nice. But, we tried to talk Chris out of it. He wasn't even divorced from number two and was already planning the wedding with number three. "Love conquers all," he would tell us with that stupid grin on his face.

To make a long story short, they got married. The second divorce finally went through. They started working together. Then they started fighting. The pattern had become predictable by this point.

After they got married, she moved in with him but things weren't working out. She told him that she needed some time to sort through things. She asked him to leave his own house for a while.

Chris is a nice guy. You could say nice to a fault. So he left. Then one day he stopped by to pick something up and found her with another guy. I guess their love conquered his.

Chris is now enjoying a fruitful life as a gym instructor. He is happily divorced, three times. He doesn't want to fall into the same trap he has been in his entire life. His closest friends are trying their hardest to keep him on a different path. So far, so good. No fourth wife. He is keeping a longtime girlfriend now, and it is healthy and it is working. She is actually perfect for him.

You know that famous saying? The definition of insanity is doing the same thing over and over and expecting different results. Well, I hope you can read between the lines enough to see when it is time to change. Change is a great thing. Embrace it with a warmest hug and softest kiss. I promise you this. It will reward you for accepting it.

Post hoc: Since this is the second edition of this book, and hopefully the last, I can happily report that Chris has decided to get hitched up. They booked a seven-day cruise that starts in Miami and goes through the beautiful Bahamas. This coming June, 2018. Those crazy kids!

"Everybody gets high, why the hell can't I?" —Missio

Chapter 10

Backpack Full of Smiles

For the last fifteen years, my friends and I have gotten together once or twice a year to just have a good time. Sometimes it's a trip with our families but on this particular trip, it was a boys' trip. Just the guys having a good time and doing exactly what it is that guys do when they get together: no good.

I'll admit, this story isn't actually about me. It's about my friend Carl, and the amazingly stupid things people do when they start "impairing their judgment."

It started down in Phoenix, Arizona on a Saturday. We were going to go to a big party that night and were in town to see my friend, Christian, who lived there. It was going to be a great time. We just didn't realize how crazy things were going to get.

In the morning, we started out with a nice round of golf. Nothing too rowdy, and we were home by 11:00 AM. Carl had started out by drinking beer in the morning. Beer is pretty mild when it comes to intoxication generally, but starting in the morning usually leads to being pretty drunk by the end of the day. But for the morning, it was just beer.

Actually, it was beer, some chewing tobacco, and then some whiskey shots. When we got back to the pool at Christian's place, Carl was ready for the weed that had appeared out of nowhere. He was on a roll.

It could be argued that each altering agent by itself wasn't too bad. But in combination, things were starting to add up. And then some of Christian's friends arrived.

These guys rolled in wearing clothes that looked like a cross between bikers and punk rockers. They wore all of the leather and spikes and had the tattoos of skulls and crossbones to show off just how hardcore they actually were. The thing is, they didn't just talk the talk. They brought their cocaine with them, and Carl wasn't ready to say "enough" yet.

After snorting a few lines, he grabbed some cigarettes and started lighting up. He must have decided that the nicotine from the chewing tobacco had worn off and he needed more in his system. To be honest, none of us were sure that he needed more of anything in his system, but we weren't ready to tell him 'no,' yet. After all, he was still functioning. His lungs were still breathing and he could carry on a conversation, even if it wasn't a very good one.

Six o'clock rolled around and Carl decided that it was time to throw something new into the chemical cocktail that was wreaking havoc on his system. The ecstasy surfaced and he decided to try it for the first time. What he didn't know was that it takes some time to work its way into your system. It wasn't working fast enough, so he took another hit.

Luckily (or not?), he was distracted by someone who came over with a bong he had appropriately named *Bertha*. It was nine feet long, and covered his entire mouth. Carl forgot about the ecstasy and stepped up to the bong.

At this point, Carl's poor, tortured body finally gave up. It was hard to say whether it was one drug kicking in, another falling off, or the combination of something else that sent him down. Either way, Carl was on the floor curled up in a little ball rocking himself back and forth.

Another friend walked in at that exact moment. He happened to be a little more conservative than Carl and the lot of us. He stared at the nine foot bong, the beers out on the counter, and the curled up man on the floor.

"He looks like a fucking newborn calf," he said in disbelief. "Guys...what the actual *fuck*?"

It was true. Carl was curled up in the fetal position, rocking and giggling to himself. I'm not sure how he managed to keep from pissing himself, he was so far gone. I started to do all the math and realized all of the drugs he had done so far that day. It didn't look good.

We hadn't even made it to the club yet.

Finally, a guy named Nick turned to me and said, "Two hundred bucks says he doesn't make it to the club tonight." Carl wasn't looking too good and the bet seemed pretty dumb. When I turned to look at Carl, he gestured for me to come over.

I walked over and leaned down. Carl was still giggling and rocking, but he must have heard what Nick said because between giggles and gasps he said three words:

"Up... tha... bet."

I looked down at Carl and saw something in his eye. I'm still not sure if it was determination or crazed stupidity. I turned to Nick and said, "Three hundred bucks and it's a bet."

I'm still not sure what happened. Like before, it could have been a drug kicking in, or another dropping off, or the perfect combination of two of them. Carl was back on his feet.

We shuffled into a few cabs and we were off to the club. We were still in the cab when one of his friends pulled out a couple of Ritalin and offered him one. It was down Carl's throat before I could even offer a protest.

That night, I won the bet. Carl made it to the club. He couldn't really walk straight, but he could walk. We had a decent time at the clubs, and Carl managed to not pass out. It was quite the accomplishment. In fact, at the end of the night, he upped the ante one last time. He was sitting at the bar and he turned to the person next to him right before we were going to leave.

"Do you have anything good hidden in your pockets?" he slurred.

One Percocet and a night cap later, we finally put him to bed.

Luckily for Carl, all he had to do the next day was get on his plane ride home. He woke up feeling the worst he had in a very long time. Hangover really isn't the word for it. He was ravaged, destroyed. And then there was the fact that any time we mentioned that day, he felt like a total ass.

I may be a D.A.R.E. graduate, but I'm not the type of person who is going to tell you *just say no*. I was by no means a poster boy for good behavior in my past. That being said, it was no small miracle that Carl didn't die or end up with a lifetime addiction. That night he got to a point where more drugs seemed to be the only thing that made sense. His judgement was impaired with a capital I. So while I won't tell you to totally avoid them, I have seen more than a few examples of why you should *watch what you do*.

Sometimes though, your only choice is to "up the bet."

"People are strange, when you're a stranger" —The Doors

Chapter 11

The Beautiful Mistakes We All Make

Have you ever had one of those jokes that just keeps going and going? This is one of those stories.

It all started with a random response to a friend at work. I told my co-workers that I was going to Portland, Oregon for the weekend and they all wanted to know why. I could have just told them that I was going to see an old friend and have some fun. It was the truth, after all. But for whatever reason, I told a lie. It was just a little lie. Or at least it was meant to be. I think I was trying to be funny but when no one caught the joke, I just ran with it.

I told them I was going to be an extra in the next *Twilight* movie.

It was a stupid lie. Really it was. But I just couldn't get past it. Someone asked how I got it lined up, and I told her that I had a friend who worked on the set. It was a total lie. She told some other people at work and by then, I couldn't just say that I made it up. Of course, it helped that none of them had seen any of the Twilight movies or really cared much about them. I told them I would send pictures.

As I left work to go to the airport, I laughed. I wasn't sure if it was at me for putting myself into such a weird position, or them for believing me.

The truth was that I was going to see George. It had been over a year since we had gotten together, and it was long overdue. When he picked me up, we went out for burgers and a drink and then got in a cab to find a bar a little closer to his place.

It was in that cab that things got messy. This next bit is not for the faint of heart... or for anyone without a sound appreciation of sixth grade boy humor.

All of the airplane food mixed with the greasy burger turned into the rankest fart that has ever escaped my poor cheeks. It smelled like a dead body had been left to rot in a dumpster next to a one star Chinese restaurant next to an alley where homeless people came to puke after drinking too much Listerine.

As soon as the potent smell hit my nostrils, I wanted to gag but clamped down on my mouth, hoping that it would be one of the farts that just stays with you. But luck was not with me that evening and a few seconds later, George turned to me with a gaping mouth and betrayed eyes. His hands fumbled desperately for the window button on the cab, but it wasn't working.

"The windows do not roll down," said our Middle Eastern cab driver in his slight accent. "It is for your safety that they are locked."

George was complaining and I was dying. It was somewhere between laughing and crying, when the noxious fumes finally hit the unfortunate cabbie.

The car swerved across a lane of traffic and screeched to a stop by the curb.

"Get the fuck out of my cab!" the man screamed.

George and I instantly sobered. "What do you mean, get out?" I asked.

"You heard me!" he said, still angry. "Get out!"

We exchanged a few choice words before George and I reluctantly crawled out of the cab, slammed the door, and walked the last few blocks to where we were staying that night.

I was dumbfounded. I had never been kicked out of a cab. Not for being rowdy. Not for being drunk. Not for being rowdy and drunk at the same time. But whatever perfect storm my bowels had brewed that evening, to our olfactory dismay, had pushed our hardened cabbie over the edge.

When we got to the hotel, George crashed, and I googled a few quick set photos from Twilight and sent them to my coworkers. There was no reason *they* needed to think my night was anything less than great.

The next night, we picked up a few more friends and went to dinner at a nice restaurant in the banking district. We didn't realize just how nice it was until we got there. From our window table, you could see out over the whole cityscape of Portland, and it was beautiful. We were lucky we got in when we did, too, because the whole place filled up rather quickly.

When the waiter brought our food, the hamburger I had ordered came out with a little wood toothpick through the top of it. We started talking and I told the guys about how I was sending home pictures I had googled and we started talking about vampires and Twilight. It didn't take too many drinks before the jokes escalated, and we were stabbing each other with the little toothpicks. They were a perfect way to stop a vampire in his tracks if he were trying to bite you. Even better than a rape whistle.

Our table was great, but we had a party to go to later that night, so we were getting ready to leave when a large, muscular black man came over to ask a favor.

He had a beautiful woman on his arm and he told us that if he gave her the special treatment and got her a good table, she would give him the special treatment later on that night.

A wink and a nod should have been enough. We should have just said sure, and let them have it. But for whatever reason, I still had vampires on the brain and before I could stop myself, I stabbed him in the chest with my little toothpick.

"Nope... not a vampire..." the words came awkwardly out of my mouth as I looked up into his eyes, hoping to not see anger.

I could have sworn that the room fell silent at that moment, and I know that all of my friends were standing there looking slack jawed at what I had just done. Luckily for me, the guy wasn't in a retributive sort of mood and he just asked me what that was about.

I awkwardly explained to him about Twilight and my coworkers and the whole joke. It didn't feel quite as funny when I told him, but he was pretty good natured about it.

When we finally got outside and on our way to the party, all of my friends let out a collective sigh of relief. We laughed for a second, and went on our way.

At the end of my vacation I returned to work, and everyone was excited for the photos and couldn't wait to see the next Twilight movie with me in it. In the end, that trip sure made me feel like the butt end of the joke, but when you're with real friends, it doesn't matter. And I like to think that it was my coworkers that felt a little bit of it when that next movie never actually made it to theaters.

"Mmm Mmm Mmm Mmm" —Crash Test Dummies

Chapter 12

Always Lawyer Up

I need to tell a bit of a somber story about a friend of mine named Shawn. Now, to be clear from the get go, Shawn is a good guy. He's a good friend and not generally this kind of stupid. But, I got permission and am telling this story because it's the type of lesson that you should learn young, and not get messed up in.

One night, Shawn, a few friends, and I went out drinking. It was a pretty typical night, or at least it started out that way. We were drinking at a place that was barely ten blocks from Shawn's place. He had parked his car at the bar and was planning on a taxi to get home, or even just walking. It was summer and it was a nice night.

When we met up at that first bar, it was just a regular night relaxing. One of the guys had to go, and the rest of us decided to head over to another bar. While we were there, we met up with another friend who we hadn't seen in quite a while, and we all got really drunk.

At that point, I took an Uber home and my friend took one back to the bar where his car was. But when he got there, the owner was there. The owner was a great guy, and none of us knew he was in town. I got a text saying that I should come back and do some shots with them.

I was already pretty wasted, and wasn't about to stay out that late. I texted him to have a good time and do a round for me. I wish I hadn't.

Shawn was pretty drunk when I left him, and I'm sure that the extra shots didn't help when it came time to go home. When he walked out of that door at almost one in the morning, he had a decision to make. It should have been a simple decision to stick to his earlier commitment and walk home.

The next morning, I heard that his brand new Hummer 2 was found parked *on top* of a Dodge Ram truck almost a block from his house.

A week later, I was drinking with one of our friends from that night and he told me he had offered to let Shawn use his lawyer. Apparently, Shawn had decided to drive home that night and totaled his new car, then had run off when the cops showed up.

The lawyer was a good one, too, because he managed to keep Shawn out of trouble and kept the cops from pinning the DUI on him even though he deserved it.

I remember talking to his wife. At first, she was horrified that I knew anything about it. Then, when I had finally convinced her that I wasn't going to rat him out, she turned furious. As it turned out, he had stumbled into the house in a drunken stagger after wrecking the car. When they finally got back outside, cops were there. She had turned to him and told him to run.

I can only imagine that he sobered up wandering the neighborhood, trying to avoid the cops in the hours before the sun came up. I do not envy him on that walk.

His wife had to lie for him and the cops tried to issue a summons to her. She told me that if it weren't for that lawyer our friend got for them, the cops probably would have worked a confession out of her.

Almost a year later, when Shawn had gotten a little more drink into him, he finally told me about that night. He told me about how he thought he could make it the ten blocks home no problem. It was stupid, and he realized it now but it's not the kind of thing you get to take back.

"It was just a few blocks," he said. "And if it weren't for my stupid phone, I never would have gotten in the wreck."

His voice was low, still looking over his shoulder to make sure that no one else was listening in.

"My phone slid across the dashboard and I reached for it. I felt a bump and the next thing I knew, I was on top of the truck. I mean, I opened the door and had to climb down the side of the fucking truck so I could stagger home. I was so stupid, man."

He told me that the lawyer said his statute of limitations was already up, but it only relieved him a little bit. It still wasn't a story he liked to tell. Insurance had taken care of the whole deal, but he still felt like he was waiting for karma to catch up with him.

Now, I'm not going to start trash talking Shawn and tell you he was a terrible person. But that one poor decision nearly cost him a whole lot. I'm still not entirely sure how he got off without the cops coming down on him. It was a combination of a tolerant, loving wife, a friend who was willing to lend him a lawyer, and stupid luck that he walked away without anything worse than a poor night's sleep and some stress. All I can say is, when you've got that decision to make, don't risk it.

"Karma is a bitch? Well just make sure that bitch is beautiful." —Lil Wayne

Chapter 13

The Sh*t You Can Buy on eBay

So pranks have been a large part of my life. I believe in humor in my life and injecting that humor, whether it's wanted or not, into the lucky people that surround me. Sometimes the pranks are innocent, sometimes they are more on the mischievous side, and sometimes they are meant to be funny but turn a little dark. This story is about the latter.

Let me start by saying there are more stories to come, in a not too distant sequel that will span the realm that makes up my brain. My wife received a beautiful homemade square-dancing dress during a Christmas visit to my parents' place. She has never square danced in her life. My buddy, George, once received a wonderful toenail painting while he was passed out. He woke up late for his flight out of Arizona. In his rush, he did not notice his beautiful new paint job until security at the airport commented on his rainbow of colors gleaming off his flip flops.

So let me preface this chapter with some back story: Carl is an old buddy of mine that loves to question the existence of life and what comes after just as much as I do. We share a fascination of paranormal and trying to reach out and see what we can find that would give us proof of some sort of life after death. We have our religious beliefs and our scientific facts working every angle of our side quest.

When Carl's mom came home one day and told us about the crazy lady she had to dispense meds to, we were not that intrigued. We were wondering why she would be telling us this story. As it turned out, she told us this crazy lady was part of a family in our city that had been notorious for being the "out there" neighbors. So much so that our local newspaper once ran a story about them and their supposed haunted house. That same paper ran another article years later after the family moved out and sent their daughter to the looney bin. That article went on to say that multiple people tried to buy the home since the family left, and they all quickly left said house within months because of activity they could not explain. Carl's mom was filling us in about the daughter that was in her psych ward. She also had details about the house, which gave way to our bad decision.

We knew the location of the home well. We drove by it all the time. This place was just like a stereotypical horror movie haunted house: three stories and a basement. Outside in disrepair. Wood panels and deck rotting away. Of course all over the house and yard were the requisite "No Trespassing" and "Trespassers will face prosecution" signs. Which was just an invitation for anyone to come on in. One stormy night, days away from Halloween, we did just that.

It took every ounce of high school courage to get to the back yard of this place. It took even more balls, and maybe a shot of stolen whiskey, to wriggle under the boarded up backdoor but in we went. The interior was actually well preserved. It did not match the dilapidation of the exterior of the home. With our flashlights on low beam, we wandered about. We started noticing empty beer and food cans. We also started to smell what could only be described as days old piss and vinegar. Disgusting for sure, but nothing was going to stop us from getting our first true ghost experience. Up the creaky old stairs we went. More empty food cans, torn up blankets, and adult magazines. This place was not giving us any haunted vibe. It was giving us the vibe that some vagrants around town had found a shelter that no one dared mess with. Until we showed up.

Up next was the basement. We knew from the articles and word of mouth around town that this is where most of the supposed activity took place. The scene was straight out of *Texas Chainsaw Massacre*. Two dumbass teenagers creeping their way into the killer's lair. The basement was indeed how it was described. A dungeon. Complete with a door in the corner that had locks, on the inside of the door. Not the outside. Odd. It was right when we were about to go into this small room that we heard the loudest crash right above us. Like two prepubescent teens hearing their first scary story during camp, we ran back up the basement stairs and right out the broken up back door. We booked it out of the yard faster than either of us could physically run.

We survived our first ghost hunt. But to no avail. It had to have been one of the homeless people returning to their den. We would go on in the next few years and try various stupid things to try and connect with the world beyond. We did Ouija board readings on gravesites in the dead of night at our local cemetery. Things like that. All to no avail. We both grew up and we both grew more skeptical that anything else was out there.

It would take about 15 more years for my first true experience (as you have read and will read) to show itself. It would take a prank on my end nearly 25 years later for Carl to get his first true experience. All thanks to eBay.

Now Brenda. She was someone I liked and admired from the first time I met her at my company's annual sales summit. Just a down to earth, no nonsense type of girl. She actually reminded me of my older sister. Just in the way she was working in a man's world but was able to not only hold her own, but become one of the top sales reps in our company. Smart, funny, and a wicked dark sense of humor. We became very good friends within our sales region and shared the same dark, witty humor.

There became a time though when it was time to turn that humor up a notch and "one up" each other in jokes. Nothing really harmful. Just little digs during conference calls and little white lies told to our teammates and co-workers that were not true, but funny none the less.

There was one day in particular she had posted an image on Facebook. She mentioned in this picture that she had come home late from a sales event and went to open her front door and automatically felt something big and furry move under her hand. Her porch light was out so she used her cell phone to shine a light on her door handle. There, in all its disgusting glory, was a ginormous tarantula. I guess it was trying to break in, but she caught it red handed. Pun intended. When I saw that disgusting pic she posted, I promptly wrote on her Facebook wall something to the effect that I hoped her insurance adjuster does not have her as a friend on Facebook as they would question why the house was burned to the ground that night. I love everything in life except for two things: spiders of any kind and dirty hippies.

She had a blast knowing I couldn't even look at a picture of a spider. To this day I still can't. Automatic shivers down my spine. So of course, what did she do? Sent me emails with attachments that would say they were work related and I would open it up and sure enough, tarantula. This went on for months until she decided to up the game, and in my opinion, the war.

It was again close to Halloween. I was gearing up for mine and my wife's first true Halloween outing with our son. I love Halloween! Just everything about it: the spooks, the costumes, and the fact that it leads into winter. Just all-around love. So it was with a little excitement that I got a nice text from my friend Brenda. She was sending me an awesome Halloween gift. One that she knew I would love. Sweet!

Two days before Halloween I get a package in the mail from Brenda. Hoping it was something cool that I could show my wife and son, I tore open the packaging paper to reveal a cool Halloween box. When I cut the tape and opened the box, my face turned pale white and I threw said box across the table. Inside were two dead, dried up tarantulas. Fucking hell. My wife looked puzzled and then aghast when she saw what it was. My two-year-old son garbled, "Cool, daddy! New pets!" My wife had a little laugh when I explained why this was sent, but I knew the prank war had just escalated. I just didn't know it would affect someone else. Whoops.

I owe somewhere around six apologies as I finish off this chapter. I just need to get that off my chest. First to Carl, his wife, and their daughter. My bad. Second, to Brenda and her sister's boyfriend. You were not supposed to open it! Jeez. Have you never seen a horror movie? Last, my wife. I kind of never told you this story until now. I know how much you believe in karma and how it all cycles back. I did not want you to think some bad juju was on the way. Truly meant as one of my famous pranks. I truly believe in karma as well and that is why I did what I had to do.

So about two years had gone by since my little spider incident. I did not forget. I just laid in wait and was biding my time to execute the perfect strike. One random, drunken Saturday night that plan was born.

You see, eBay is a wonderful tool and an even better concept. You can purchase almost anything on its site and sell with impunity. It's also a glorious model for true market demand. You pay or sell only what people truly want. My plan actually was born when I sold something that I couldn't fathom someone wanted, on eBay.

When we had our little incidents at our prior home, I was sure of where that energy came from. We had gotten some very old artifacts from recently deceased family members on my wife's side of the family. Ava's aunt and uncle had stopped by our place and told us we could have a few boxes of various pictures, jewelry boxes, and artifacts as they did not have the room to store it. We reluctantly agreed and went on with life. Well sort of. Unexplainable things occurred around this same time period and I was tired of them. In my internet research I found some stories from others that they figured out where said energies were from: old artifacts. It was time for ours to go. So I just happened to look up "haunted" in my eBay search. It returned a crap load of items that were for sale that had supposed energy attached to them. eBay, rightfully so, said these were not guaranteed by them and owners are at their own risk. Made sense. So instead of dumping said items, I felt that the energy might want to find another home. They did. They were auctioned off and I could not believe the amount of money we made off these "haunted items." Hence my next actions in the prank war.

I had been watching some supposed "haunted" items the last few months and just didn't feel the prank war had that high of a price. Until I happened upon an interesting "Dybbuk box". This was interesting. It came from a young gentleman who supposedly decided he no longer wanted to be in the realm of the living. So he made an interesting box, carved up some weird symbols, sealed said box, and traveled into the famed Aokigahara forest to end his life. Later, when someone happened upon his decaying remains, they took some items, the Dybbuk box being one of those. The box made its way into a few different hands and then ended up on eBay. I made an incredibly high offer of twenty dollars and it was taken the second I sent it over. Cool that they wanted to get rid of it so quickly.

Now here is where the plot thickens. I didn't want something like that in my house. My wife would *kill* me! Plus, I couldn't send it from Colorado. Even with no return address it would be post marked originating from Colorado. Brenda would know right away. So I had to think real hard about where I could go with it that she would never suspect a thing.

That's when my paranormal past explorations with Carl came to mind. He had shifted strictly to the "paranormal is bullshit" realm, even after I told him my experiences. This would be perfect. I could have the eBay seller ship to Carl's address in Maine, and then he could ship it on to Brenda. No return address and post marked from Maine. Nothing to come back to Colorado. Also, if the thing was really haunted, Carl would get his first true experience. If not, I just threw away twenty dollars on a very ornate box. Great antique gift for Brenda.

So with no explanation, I had the box shipped to Carl. Between shipping time and life, I actually kind of forgot I had done that. Two weeks after said transaction, I get a call from Carl. He had gotten a weird box delivered to him and it came from Florida. He somehow knew that I would be involved. So I told him the story, the prank, and what I needed him to do. He laughed, then he turned serious. He was a little concerned as he had a new wife and daughter living with him. He did not want to involve them. I told him to grow up. Besides, he had already proven to himself that this stuff was all bullshit. He laughed again and agreed to get it out the next day.

Here is the thing though. Carl? Awesome dude. Super fun and overall a very kind heart. The one thing he did not have going for him was his ability to actually get things done in a timely fashion. I may, or may not, have known that when I picked him to be the receptacle of said gift. True to form, when I asked him if he got the box shipped off to Brenda, he said he was super busy with his PlayStation and football games. He just forgot about it. I told him no problem, just get it out as soon as possible. I also told him whatever he did, do not open it. He laughed, called me an idiot, and went back to watching *Step Up*, a fantastic movie with Channing Tatum.

Exactly two days later I get a call from Carl. Sweet. He finally mailed out my little prank. Or so I thought. Nope. He was all in huff and seemed off from his usual self.

"Fuck dude. I was sitting down to dinner with my wife and kid last night. Our kitchen is right below our master bedroom. All three of us were just talking when we heard a huge bang above us, followed by multiple footsteps. We were sure that we had an intruder that had somehow broken through our bedroom window. I told the girls to grab the phone and get ready to dial the cops. I took out a butcher knife and went to confront the burglar upstairs. When I got up there, it was completely empty. Window was shut and locked. That fucking box was just sitting there in the corner. The fuck dude. Why did you send me that shit?" he bellowed.

I went on to tell him that I didn't want that shit in my house. Fuck that. But glad he might have found some proof of the other side. So cool!!

"Fucking Asshat!" He hung up on me.

The next day I got a text from him that said he had dropped it off with his shipping manager at his company's warehouse. Finally. Two weeks later I would start to get my revenge. Thanking him for finally getting around to it and apologizing that I sent it to him, I was relieved it was going to my intended target. Or so we both thought.

Turns out, Carl and his wife left the next day for vacation. When he got back two weeks later and went back to work he found the box, still packaged, sitting on his desk. WTF? He thought. He set it aside and when lunch rolled around he ran down to the warehouse. "Why did Darryl not deliver this?", he thought to himself on the way there. He found out why. Apparently the day after he dropped it off, Darryl, who had been with the company almost 12 years, up and quit. No one knows why. No one talked to Darryl. He just quit. Strike two for the box?

To be fair to me here, I did tell Carl to go to the post office and mail it right away. I even told him I would cover all costs. Good ol' Carl though, never one to pass up on an easy way out. He thought he would save us both some money, and him some time, and have his warehouse ship it. Whoops.

Carl finally had enough. He got it shipped, again through his warehouse, and made sure it was on the truck out. Finally. The prize was on its way to the true recipient.

As it turns out, by the time it was headed to Brenda's house, she was already on a plane to Greece for a two-week vacation with friends and family. The package arrived. Her sister's boyfriend was taking care of mail and general upkeep while they were all away. So in the house it goes.

Once again I had almost forgotten about my two year prank until I got a random text from Brenda.

"Hey, did you send me a random box?" the text simply stated.

"No. What are you talking about? Did something come from my home address?" I lied back with complete satisfaction and a bit of the giggles. My wife was staring at me oddly.

"Well, no. I got this weird box, with all these creepy carved symbols all over it. It came from Maine. But I thought for some reason you might have sent it?"

We went back and forth and I got her to describe it to me a little more. I played dumb and finally told her it was probably a gift from her family or something like that. She promptly said she knew no one in the Maine area and what was even weirder was that it had no return address. She was smart enough to figure out the Fed Ex tracking code though.

Fucking Carl. You dumbass.

She then went on to tell me how she already found the company it came from, and that she was calling their HR department to demand to know who it came from. I felt a little bad for Carl at this point. I was pretty sure he would not get in trouble for using the company funds for his buddy's jokes, but I thought I would give him a heads up anyhow. I also tried to negotiate with Brenda to send the supposed haunted box to another one of my friends. I tried telling her it would be funny and I would pay for it. She was having none of it. She said she wouldn't touch the box and it was already out on her porch for immediate pick up. Guess she scared the Fed Ex people into immediate action. LOL?

I left it alone. I let Carl know what was going on. He laughed. He said it would be no issue and it would not come back to him. Sure enough, he was right.

About a year goes by and this story is never mentioned. Then about a month ago, prior to the release of this book, I got a text from a buddy of mine. This buddy of mine still works with Brenda. He was just doing me a solid and proofreading what you all have in your hands. He randomly sent me a text and asked if I had told Brenda about the haunted box prank. I forgot I told him about the prank. I knew I was going to include this story. I wasn't sure if it was going to make this book or if it was the next. In this case, it was time to let that curious cat out of the proverbial bag.

I hadn't chatted with Brenda a lot since the haunted box incident. Busy lives. I sent her a random text telling her I had to tell her something but she had to promise that she wouldn't lose it. I involved my buddy because they were both at the same sales summit.

So I sent Brenda a text back that gave her strict directions. If she wanted the information I had for her, she was to write a note, third grade style, and pass it along up to said buddy. The note was to read: "Chance told me. I can't believe you knew and didn't tell me. I thought we were friends. That could have killed me." She then had to take two pictures: one of my buddy opening the note and then of his face and reaction when he turns and looks at you. Like a true champ, she did it. The pictures I got back were priceless! She earned her reward.

I spilled the beans. Her reaction was spot on.

"I knew it was fucking you!! Asshole!!" she texted back in all caps.

I then went on to explain my stance and how she started it all with the dead tarantulas. I let her know that at least she didn't have the guys walking around her house like my buddy did who had the demon box before her.

That's when the prank took a little detour. She laughed at Carl's story, but then she texted me back.

"Ever since getting that damn box, some odd experiences have come into my life. My bank account had over 20k illegally transferred out. My credit card was stolen and my Verizon account was hacked. I called a priestess and had my house cleansed of all evil presences, after I returned that stupid box. I found out my sister's boyfriend had opened the box while he was taking care of my house. I got all the shit taken care of. Money replaced. Cards cancelled. My sister's boyfriend had taken pictures of it when he opened it. He knew a mystic lady in Austin and took the pictures to her. She said all signs on the box were positive. No curses. All of it means well," she texted back.

We laughed about some of it and that made me feel a little better. Geez. I just wanted some creepy sounds or the thought of some weird stuff happening. All random coincidence. Very random it all happened around the same time as said box arrived and left.

I can happily report that all is well in her life. She won Sales Manager of the year. Her house is as happy as ever. No signs of darkness or doom. Still a shit ton of tarantulas nesting in her back yard and under her house.

One last thing to report. Carl? We met up here very recently. Did a small guys' trip to visit one of our longtime friends that just found out he had leukemia. Sad, but happy to report my friend is doing well. As we got to telling stories late the first night we were all together, this story was brought up. Carl stopped laughing.

"You know, we got a new dog recently. That dog is awesome. But there have been multiple times now where it goes into the corner of our room and just growls at the corner. The corner where that damn box sat. He just sits there and stares and growls" he said.

Kids. Don't mess with dad. I am the king of pranks. Enough said.

"Where ya going with the mask I found?" —Stone Temple Pilots

Chapter 14

Weenie Roasting Furries

Sometimes things work out just right, bringing the stars into alignment in a way that leaves you speechless. Sometimes, life is just a perfect shit storm where everything goes horribly wrong. And sometimes life throws you something in between, a moment so strange that you couldn't make it up if you wanted to.

I had just gotten a new job and they wanted to train me in California. That was fine by me. I knew George was going to be in California around the same time and convinced my company to give me an extra day as long as I covered the hotel expenses for the extra night. It was a small price to pay for a chance to catch up with George.

As an added bonus, one of George and I's good friends from high school happened to be living in the Orange County area, which was mere miles from where we were staying. We reached out to her and made a very loose commitment to all try and get together.

Then to top things off, Weenie Roast was going to be that weekend. It was a big music festival in Irvine and we were going to be just down the street from it. When I was boarding the plane, George called to tell me he would try and get tickets for us if he could stay with me in my hotel. Perfect.

The flight was uneventful and as soon as I landed, George called. There weren't any tickets left, but it was still going to be a good time. He also sounded like he was trying to be mysterious about something. I tried to get it out of him, but the most he would say was, "You'll see when you get here. I'll be in the bar."

When I arrived at the hotel, it was obvious that something was going on. First off, parked out in the parking lot were a bunch of huge tour busses. Most of the big bands for Weenie Roast were staying in the same hotel with us! In fact, as I walked in the hotel, I passed Scott Weiland (now deceased lead singer for the Stone Temple Pilots) as he was going out to their tour bus. That would have been impressive enough were it not for the fact that I ran into a truly weird sight in the lobby.

Inside the lobby and in the bar, there were *hundreds* of people dressed up in animal costumes.

When I found George in the bar, he told me that all of the bands for Weenie Roast were staying here. "And there's a Furry Con here this weekend," he said nonchalantly.

"A what?" I asked.

"A Furry Convention, that's all I know" he said. "It's kind of a big deal, I guess."

I shook my head and looked around. It was hard to say exactly what it looked like. My first thought would have been a mascot convention.

Imagine being at Six Flags Magic Mountain in California and going to Bugs Bunny World. You'd see all of your favorite anthropomorphic cartoon characters portrayed by people in big animal suits, and you might get your kids to stand next to one as you take their picture. Then you go back to your hotel, and they're all at the bar, drinking. Oh, and now there are about a hundred more of them that you don't recognize. It was like that.

There were a lot of dog-like masks. Some wore full body suits, while others just settled for the mask and sleeves under their normal clothes. They were every color of the rainbow, from bright purple to orange with white spots.

It was at that point that my friend Susan called to tell us that she would meet us at the beach in a couple of hours. That sounded just perfect. George and I would get to hang out with our old friend, but until then, we got to explore. George and I had a drink and then began to wander through the different rooms that were open for the Furry Convention guests.

In a lot of ways, it was just like a lot of other conventions. There were booths where people were selling art crafts and different books and products. There were rooms with classes about Furries. For example, did you know that as a Furry, you need to earn the right to wear your costume? I didn't. There was a darkened room full of Furries in chairs, watching Speedy Gonzales cartoons.

But in other ways, it was definitely different. George and I went separate ways for a bit, but when we met back up, he showed me something that I'm still not quite sure how to interpret. In a room that was kind of tucked away in a corner, there was a bunch of costumed individuals in a circle around two particular Furries. They were having sex. I'm still not sure about the logistics of it. I'm pretty sure they had holes in their costumes, but either way, I wasn't about to stay and investigate. It was odd to say the least.

We walked out of the room and I checked my watch, hoping that it would be time for us to leave for the beach. It was close enough. We hailed a cab and away we went to our next adventure.

We met up with Susan, who told us that her husband knew the general manager at a fancy steak house near the beach, so we could go there and eat a free dinner later. It sounded good to us.

It wasn't until we got to this steak house that we realized exactly the sort of place it was. Mastro's Ocean Club. It was a 5-star steak house that didn't spare any expense. This place was *nice*.

It was a shame that her husband was exactly the sort of person you would expect to see there.

Susan's husband was big. No, that doesn't quite do him justice. The guy was a meathead. You know that one guy at your gym? The one who has the tattoos that he thinks make him look totally badass? The one who uses so many steroids that you wonder if he's doing it on purpose as an alternative to birth control? That is the guy we met when we walked in. I don't remember his name, but we'll refer to him as Dick.

In Dick's defense, the dinner was great. Fancy place. He and his friends were actually including us into their conversations. When we were done, we all sat at the glass bar on our fancy transparent stools, getting drunk. When we each had enough alcohol to be a bit wobbly, Dick pulls out some chewing tobacco and offers it around.

So neither George nor I normally chew, but only I was smart enough to turn him down.

It took George about five whole minutes before he started to gag on the chaw and his body decided it was rejection time. Before any of us were able to realize what was happening, George leaned over the packed bar and spat out the oversized wad of chaw into a freshly made Mojito. WTF??!!

The bartender and a couple of the waiters froze and just stared at the cup on the counter. One of the waiters started to walk over to us, but Dick caught his eye and shook his head.

"People usually get arrested for stunts like that," Dick said, leaning over to George. "I think it's time for you guys to go."

George looked at Dick, saw the way his shirt pulled tight against his chest and arms, and wisely refrained from making a fuss as he stood up to leave. I watched the exchange, let out a sigh, and got up from my chair as well.

Dick and Susan did not quite have their fill of our antics. Yet. Susan, being the good friend, suggested that we all head over to the South Coast Plaza. Just a walk away. Maybe George would sober up a little. Little did they know we were a package deal that night.

Susan got the crew up to the rooftop bar above Saks Fifth Avenue. She told George and myself to go find a spot for all of us out on the patio. She would order our drinks and calm down Dick and his buddies. George and I were still joking as we headed for the door. I'm not sure if I was too drunk or just not paying attention, but regardless, I plowed into and knocked over a table. The translucent table top shimmied for a brief moment before it hit the ground and shattered into a million little glass shards. It was all in clear HD slow motion.

I started to glance around and saw just how nice everything really was. Every bit of furniture was all made of glass. The tables, the bar, the chairs. All of it was beautifully clear and shiny. Well, except for the one I had just body checked.

Dick ran over and started pushing us until we were out the door, probably hoping that no one had associated us with him, preserving his bulging reputation from such tarnish. When Susan turned to see what had happened, I just instinctively pointed towards George and made a gesture to say, "Wasn't me, it was him!"

Apparently that rooftop bar no longer has glass anything for decor. Anywhere. Thanks a lot, George.

We said goodbye to the group after that literal walk of shame. With our heads high up in the air we strolled through Saks Fifth like men on a mission. It was nine PM and we had a lot more time to find the next adventure.

When we got back, it was really hard to not laugh. Our next adventure was waiting for us. We walked in through the bar and saw almost all of the seats occupied. Every other seat was filled with neon colored animal costumes. The other half were every kind of punk rocker you can imagine. It was comical. I almost expected them to start dancing and snapping their fingers in some strange adaptation of West Side Story.

George and I wandered through the crowd and talked to people. George was about ready to pass out, and it didn't take much before he left to go back to the room. I, on the other hand, got to talk to some of the coolest people around. I shared a beer with some guys from Papa Roach. I got to shoot the breeze with some other bands that were trying really hard to make it. And over in the corner, there was a skinny white guy who looked like he was crazy high. He was leaning heavily against a giant fox to remain standing. It was Scott Weiland.

When I finally got back to the room, George was out cold. I looked again at the amazing pictures on my phone, and then joined him.

"Alcohol may be man's worst enemy, but the bible says love your enemy." —Frank Sinatra

Chapter 15

Fly Me to the Moon

There are times in your life when you are stuck, mentally or physically, somewhere or on something. When you find yourself in one of those places, take the time and just be. Learn something.

It was a beautiful early May morning in the northern Sierra Nevada Mountains. My parents had come to Roseville, California to visit and they had brought along my niece, their granddaughter. We had just finished a trip to Napa Valley, and my mom was a little worse for wear. I know exactly where I get my love of alcohol from.

It was a little over two hours from Roseville to Lake Tahoe. We were headed up for the day. We wanted to take a spin around Lake Tahoe and maybe stop by a curiosity shop.

It was great company, although my poor niece was probably a little uncomfortable with it all. The owners of the last couple of vineyards we visited the day before gave her the wink and the nod, and she got to have a little "wine time" with her grandparents, crazy uncle, and one of my even crazier friends.

We were making our gradual ascent into the heavily forested, still snowcapped Sierra Mountains when my Mom got excited. "Oh, yeah," she said. "I have a great idea! We should go check out Frank Sinatra's old haunt Cal-Neva!" She and my father always have fondly remembered their up-close and personal concerts they attended to see Frank Sinatra and Elvis, the rock gods of their era.

It was a perfect idea. It would be an easy stop on the north side of Tahoe before we drove along the east shore down to South Lake Tahoe. We could even do some gambling. Besides, if my mom wanted to do something, which was not often, she said it and we did it.

We got directions and followed them until we found ourselves driving down the long ramp to the hotel. Looking at it, we figured it probably had not been updated since Sinatra passed, which only made it even more awesome.

These were the hallowed halls where the Rat Pack (a group of super popular actors and crooners including Frank Sinatra) had enjoyed many, many crazy nights, not unlike the one we spent there. But I'd be willing to bet that there were probably a lot more booze, drugs, and nakedness.

As we took a look at the hotel, wandering around and checking out its history, we noticed some large flakes of snow coming down. These weren't the random, sleet, wet flakes you get this time of year.

Still, no big deal, we thought. It was early May, and snow is common that time of year there. We spent the next hour messing around the hotel letting my mom and dad get their fill of nostalgia, while my poor niece watched. At least George and I were able to grab some free cocktails and throw a few bucks down on the tables. But all the while those snowflakes were getting bigger and the storm was growing thicker.

We decided that after the long drive and the tour, it was about time for some well-deserved lunch. We meandered into the only restaurant that doubled as a lounge. Despite being a Saturday afternoon, it was not at all crowded. There were a few families, some older couples, some stragglers, and us. Cal Neva had seen better times.

We started ordering and spitting out old stories, but still didn't realize how hard the snow had gotten in the two hours since we arrived. We somehow missed the two and a half feet of fluffy, compacting snow.

It was about an hour into our very long lunch that my niece told us that we should check out the window. It was then that we finally saw the total white out that was outside.

It was very quickly becoming evening. It was time to get our check and go. But, as we started walking out the front of the hotel, we saw the few staff members shoveling. They were working hard to try and clear off the walk but they were barely making a dent.

And then there was the road up to the main highway. It was freshly snowed over, and had not been plowed at all.

Ok, we thought. No big deal. We'll just head back in and wait for the snow to stop.

It didn't stop. All damn night.

It was around 6:00 PM we knew that we would not be leaving that night. For most of us, that was awesome. All my poor niece had was some end of the year high school paper that she had to finish.

My parents grabbed a room for themselves and my niece and my wife, George, and I got a double queen bed room to ourselves. Luckily, the hotel wasn't very full and my parents were able to get us a discount. George and I made some calls to our work to let them know where we were and we all settled in to enjoy the snow.

My mom was tired and ready to go to bed early, so she quickly volunteered to stay with my niece. My wife, dad, George, and I all decided to go try our luck in Frank Sinatra's pit. This had to be a sign from above, right? We had to be here for a reason, and each of us was about to find out what it was. Each of us started gambling on our own. My wife went to some slots, won some money, and then joined us for a few rounds at the Blackjack table. My dad did his own thing but also eventually joined us all at the Blackjack table. George and me? We went to the Blackjack table and made immediate friends with the pit boss.

Now, there are two things you should know. First, George, even though he was barely twenty-eight at the time, had a knack of making best friends with people much older than himself. It was a very endearing quality. Everyone loved the guy. But old folks? Oh, they fell in love immediately, and he loved every second of it. He knew how to talk to them and how to joke with them. It was the weirdest superpower ever, but it fit George like a glove.

And second, it is my firm belief that everybody loves me. If they don't, they just need a little more time and a double dose of my over-the-top humor.

We were about to embark on the second case of red wine, and were well into our "fun" mode. Through some strange twist of fate, George and I were both winning. That never happened. It was always one or the other. And more often than not, both of us blew our winnings by pushing our luck and not just walking away.

As a little bit of advice, learn to walk away when you're up.

By the time my father and wife came over to our table, we had not only won a fair amount of cash, we had also made lifelong friendships with the people at our table, the staff, and more importantly, Frank Sinatra's old pal the Pit Boss.

We were far beyond simple pleasantries at this point. We were talking about each other's families, and got to hear the pit boss' stories of his year with Mr. Sinatra. Where was my mom now? I thought. Is this what she had guided us here for? At least pops got to hear all the old stories and throw in his two cents.

The pit boss was about four years older than my dad. They, of course, understood each other and their generation. The red wine kept flowing; it was part of the gambling table's ploy. They needed you drunk to make those bad decisions, and we were about to open the final case of red wine...

Three hours later, my wife had left and the people who remained at the tables were finding their own excuses for getting drunk.

I had progressed beyond fun into what my friends call "crossing wires." I would love to blame it all on the booze but the truth is, I just had a pre-disposition for mixing drunken stupor with my own "witty" humor.

It had been all fine and dandy earlier. But now, the pit boss was watching me become sloppy. Even worse, I was being sloppy with Frank's buddy. My dad tried stopping me multiple times, and George was trying to figure out how he had lost a thousand dollars in the last seven hours. It was right about then that I finally pushed the pit boss too far.

I called him, "Dawg". *My* Dawg to be exact. There's obviously more to the story, but what mattered at the moment was that last comment broke the camel's back.

The man was about seventy and had obviously put up with many, many unpleasant situations in his time between Vegas and Lake Tahoe. The Rat Pack were known for their exploits. But somewhere along the line, I had crossed over to the realm of "done".

I think my father saw it first. The pit boss looked at me and said, "Your time here is done, and let's not further date that rejection time." Out of respect for the workers and the customers, my dad decided that the pit boss was correct. It was time to escort his son out, with the help of the two security guards who had also been snowed in with us.

George watched my Dad take me by the arm and sternly guide me away from the table and back to the elevator and stairs to get back to our room. I'll admit that I don't really remember much of it. I remember vague glimpses of some big dudes helping my dad, my dad clutching my belt in one hand, my other arm draped around him, and my slow, drunken protest as we made our way back to the room.

My wife awoke with some heavy knocks to our hotel room door. She groaned.

Those dumbasses lost their keys or left them in here, she thought.

In her defense, it would have been par for the course. But tonight was a tad bit different. There was her husband, or a slobbering mess that resembled him, slung over his father's arm along with what she could only assume were Kanye West's bodyguards flanked on each side.

"Ava," my dad said, very matter-of-factly, "It's time for Chance to go to bed." That was all that was ever needed between my wife and my father. I was hustled into bed, the only thing I really remember was her voice telling me to, "keep it down, we have neighbors."

I was completely out when she heard some odd noises, about five minutes later. It was like a bear, she told me later, emptying a garbage can looking for food: the same grunts and same sounds. She blindly called out in the dark, and heard a voice she knew. It was George.

"Hey Avaaaaa," came his slurred voice. "I followed Chance up after the pit boss kicked him out, and got lost for a moment. I know I hid some of my earlier winnings somewhere."

Ava turned on the night lamp next to the bed. There was George in a completely disheveled state with his overnight bag turned upside-down, shaking it like a crack addict looking for that last high.

"George, get ahold of yourself," she said. "If you lost all of your money, then maybe it's time to call it quits."

"But Ava" he said in what he probably thought was very clear-headed logic, "I hid my 'ups' in here knowing I would need them later. I know I can win it all back. I'm just looking for my 'C' note."

My wife was pretty fed up with it at this point and told him, "Well get it, and get the hell out. Its 3:00 in the fricking morning and still dumping snow, and my husband was just dropped off by his dad. Time to call it quits or get the eff out."

With that not-so-subtle hint, George gave up his task of finding those hidden 'ups', and collapsed into his bed. Luckily for him, he would find his 'C' notes in the next couple of days and make up for some of the large loss he had incurred down in Sinatra's old pit with Sinatra's old friend.

The next morning we all got up and headed down to the only open restaurant there. It had snowed so much that no one had left, not even the employees. Sinatra's old friend was still in his tux from the night before. He noticed us all as we were heading to the restaurant.

"Hey, you assholes," he said, obviously tired. He was not amused. I was afraid that some of my still-fuzzy, belligerent behavior was about to be brought up in front of everyone in the restaurant. He walked like a man possessed up to George and I. My wife moved away from me like I just had contracted the plague.

"You dumb fucks," he said. "I didn't know it was even possible. You two assholes thought, and probably told everyone, that you were wine seawards or vintners. You ended up drinking out the entire bar and kitchen of red wine. With being snowed in and the highways being limited up here, we won't have our next shipment until next weekend."

He gave me a loud slap on the back, gave my dad a wink, and a hit on his arm. "Actually I am damn impressed either of you are up and alive today. The last time I saw that happen was a wild night I was stuck with Frank and Sammy. They got into the wine real heavy, like you two idiots. They almost had to cancel the next two nights of performances. Thank god they were functioning alcoholics."

"So I guess a glass of gin to wash away this raging headache might not happen?" I wearily said.

It's all I could do but smile as he turned around and flipped us off all the way to the kitchen. Frank's old friend was genuine to the last day on this earth.

"At home, drawing pictures, of mountain tops, with him on top" —Pearl Jam

Chapter 16

No Need for Batteries

At this point in my life, it seems like I have had more close shaves with death than with my Gillette razor. I look back at them with mixed feelings; sometimes with awe and wonder at my own stupid luck. Sometimes it's just gratitude to have missed what seemed to have been coming for me once again.

It gets me really thinking about just how fortunate we are to be alive, despite the fact that we wake each morning to take up the slow march towards the day of our inevitable death. It's enough to make anyone depressed were it not for the fact that those days in between can be so much fun.

When those close shaves actually come, the moments that remind you of your own mortality, it's often not the big decisions that make the difference. It's the little things.

The year was 2012. The Olympics were about to start up in London and the UN was trying unsuccessfully to get Iran to stop trying for nuclear power. But you know what I was really excited about?

Batman.

When I was thirteen I saw the first Batman movie, and it changed my life. Righteous vengeance, genius detective work, and overcoming evil all wrapped up into a one-man, crime-fighting caped crusader. When I saw that movie, it rocked my world and inspired me. In fact, I went to the barber and had him shave the bat sign into the back of my head.

You can imagine exactly how my parents reacted to *that* little stunt. But, I didn't care. I wanted to let the world know that I was proud of

Batman. He was doing the right thing. He was badass as hell, and I was too.

So when Christopher Nolan came along with Batman Begins, I caught a glimpse of perfection. It was the type of performance that gives you the chills. Little did I know that there was one more element that needed to be added to the mix: Heath Ledger.

When I went to see The Dark Knight midnight showing with my wife, I felt transformed back into my thirteen-year-old self all over again.

With that single, brilliant movie came the most insane, perfect mixture of art and reality that I had ever seen. Heath Ledger's portrayal of the Joker would become the embodiment of pure evil in a way that no one had ever seen. He inspired a generation of memes, quotes, and people: one of whom would almost cost me my life.

It was all my wife could do to convince me that a thirty-year-old man did not need to shave that bat symbol back into my head.

Meanwhile, I had taken another long dive into the corporate world to help support my family and had been working for Capital One for the last two years. Like most corporate jobs, this one had its ups and downs. Pay was good, and my family was doing pretty good with it. Hours were sometimes a little excessive, but you know how it is. You deal with it or you leave.

But while the rest of the world was getting ready to watch the world's greatest athletes, there was only one hero that I couldn't wait to see. The Dark Knight Rises was set to come out on July 27th and I was counting down the days.

The entire month of July, there was nothing I would rather talk about. You know that guy in the office who seems to be obsessing *way* too much over the tiniest bits of trivia about some imaginary something or other? The one that won't let you get a word in edgewise because he is so excited? You know. That guy who has talked about this movie so much that you're almost convinced to go see it? That was me.

I know. I can feel your judgement, just like I could feel theirs. I had my freaky Batman flag out and I was letting it fly. I would talk about the character, and how this iteration compared to the different directors and the comics and cartoons. I speculated endlessly with the rest of the internet about what exactly was going to be Nolan's take on the different characters, and ogled the leaked set pictures. Anyone who would give me the time of day would end up with way more than they bargained for.

As the day of the premier drew closer, I got more and more excited. My wife had set me up perfectly to have an amazing experience. She was taking my son and her sister up to spend some time with her mom just south of Yellowstone National Park. That meant that for the night of the premier of the most anticipated movie of my entire adult life, it was going to be just me and my brother-in-law.

Plans for the night? Simple. Get a little tipsy and then go watch the cinematic event of the year.

Well, ok. Not just that simple. I called him up and tried to convince him to come to my place. My little town in south Denver had a great, state-of-the-art theater and we could crash at my house afterwards. Seemed like a good idea until he reminded me that there was a theater just six blocks from his place.

We could drink at his house, get nice and tipsy, and then just walk to the theater. Then walk back. No driving required. That was just about perfect. Why hadn't I thought of that?

The next day, we met up to buy tickets. It was pretty close to opening night, and we were a little worried that there wouldn't be any tickets left. Luckily for us, there were still a few. We had caught a break and were excited, choosing our seats and getting ready to buy them. My brother-in-law was about to click that beautiful little green "Buy Now" button when I felt a shiver go down my spine.

Have you ever had one of those moments where it almost seems like someone is trying to page you from the great beyond? And the pager just happens to be attached to your spinal cord? That's kind of what this was like. It was completely unmistakable, and utterly unforgettable.

At the time, all I could think to say was, "Hold up a sec. I just need to check my schedule." My brother-in-law just gave me a look that said: you've been ranting about this movie for the past two months and you just now think to check your schedule.

But it was a good thing I did, because there it was staring at me from my phone. My thirteen-year-old brain had gotten so excited about the movie that it had forgotten to check in with my work-going, semi-responsible adult brain. That next morning at 9:00 AM, I had a meeting with a client for work and it wasn't the kind of meeting I could miss.

I did the math. The movie was at 12:00 midnight. That meant that it would be over around 3:00 AM. Fort Collins, where the meeting was, was two hours away. That meant going to bed around 4:00 AM and getting up at 6:00 AM so I could leave by 7:00 AM and get there by 9:00 AM. Two hours of sleep. Had I been a young and dumb twenty-something-year-old, I might have tried it but my thirty-something self was a little reluctant. Sleep deprivation wasn't as much fun as it had seemed in college.

So with heavy heart, I told my brother-in-law to hold up. I told him to not buy the tickets. I had somewhere to be.

He just stared at me.

I would just have to wait for the weekend like everyone else. There was no way around it.

Thursday morning, I woke up and thought about the movie that I wouldn't be going to see that night. Being an adult had never seemed so depressing. I decided to go up to Fort Collins to see if I could get my mind off of Batman by driving into work.

I spent the day working on business, trying to ignore the crying thirteen-year-old inside me. Luckily, the client heard that I was in town and asked if he could take me and some of his top employees to dinner that night. He wasn't Batman, but it was better than nothing.

Actually, it was *way* better than nothing because he took us to Sonny Lubick's Steak House. This place was spectacular. Sonny was a coach for CSU who raised the bar for their football team and led them to six conference titles and set numerous other records during his tenure there.

When we were done, the client asked if we could move our meeting back a bit the next morning. I readily agreed, already feeling a little bit woozy. In the back of my mind, a thirteen-year-old was complaining that I could have made it to my movie, but luckily the alcohol made it hard to hear him.

And it was about to get worse.

The employees I was with were having a great time and asked if I wanted to tour some of the historic bars with them. I was tipsy, but when a client wants to schmooze you, you don't say no. So off we went.

Fort Collins is a funny town. It's not Boulder, but don't let that fool you. It is a college town through and through. Within a mile radius, there are no fewer than thirty bars of every type. There were lounges, dive bars, burger bars, patio decks, and everything else. Well, almost everything else, because we never once ran into a sports bar. Sure, there were a few small TVs in the back of a few of the bars, but nothing big. Nothing that was meant for public use. And what did I care? I was there to have a good time.

The folks I was with met up with some friends and we started drinking. We started sipping mojitos and that led to slamming Moscow mules. It didn't take too long before it was getting late enough that the crowds were starting to thin out. Things started to get blurry and before I even realized it, it was time to head home.

I staggered out, following the light of the bright green sign of the Garden Hilton where I was staying, climbed up to my room, and stumbled through the door. As I landed my bed, I glanced at the little red digital clock beside my bed: 3:00 AM.

It is 3:00 AM. How the fuck is it 3:00 AM? You could have just gone to the movie, an angry thirteen-year-old voice inside my head screamed. I was so mad. Tomorrow was going to be coming really quick. I brushed my teeth, downed a cup of water, and set my alarm for what I knew was going to feel like a mere blink later. With that done, I promptly proceeded to pass out into the hotel bed.

Two hours later, my phone went off.

I rolled over and glared at it, sitting next to an angry red clock readout that said, 5:04 AM. Who was calling at five in the morning? I wondered, disoriented. No one for me, that's who, I silently answered. I went back to sleep.

My work phone went off again minutes later. Then my personal phone. Then the work phone again. Then both of them at the same time. Finally, about thirty minutes later I was angry enough to sit up and try to figure out what was going on.

I shook my head, trying to clear out the grogginess when suddenly, a thought hit my brain like a ton of bricks: My wife and son.

I picked up my work phone, glancing at all the missed calls.

"What!?!" I yelled into the phone. "Did I miss the meeting we *didn't* schedule to have at 5:30 AM?"

"Chance! Is that you?" came a worried voice from the other end. "Are you alright?" It was Wes, one of my teammates.

"No, I'm not alright!" I yelled back into the phone. "I went to bed three hours ago and I'm hung over. What is so important that it couldn't wait until later?"

"Chance, have you seen the news?"

"Not since yesterday," I said, a little confused. There hadn't been anything out of the ordinary then.

"Chance, there was a shooting in Denver. At the Batman movie."

That night, in Aurora, Colorado, James Holmes walked into a theatre dressed in a tactical vest and started throwing gas canisters. Then he opened fire using handguns and shotguns on the crowd, killing twelve and injuring another seventy. In the end, he would be sentenced to twelve consecutive life sentences and 3,318 years without parole.

It finally occurred to me just how worried everyone must be.

They knew that I loved Batman. They had heard me talk about almost nothing else. They knew that I had planned to be at the midnight showing, and they had no way of checking my calendar to see that I had gone to a meeting instead. And the shooting had occurred in Denver.

They were right to be scared.

But, they weren't nearly as scared as I was, because I knew the truth. I knew exactly where that Cinema 16 was. It was twenty-five miles from my house in Highlands Ranch. It was about six blocks from where my brother-in-law lived. I was supposed to be there.

To this day, I'm not sure why I got that shiver down my spine. I'm not sure why it inspired me to check my calendar, of all things. And I'm not sure why it was that I was working for Capital One, the company that had a client who would set up a meeting for that particular Friday morning. I could have blown off the meeting. I could have totally spaced it. I might have gotten in a little trouble, but no one could have blamed me. I could have been one of the four hundred people crammed into that theater when James Holmes walked in. But for some chance of fate, I wasn't.

"Take my hand, we'll make it I swear" —Bon Jovi

Chapter 17

Divorced at 23, 29, and 36

Chance J.J. Edric. My other half, my husband, the father to my children, my love, my "you complete me" man of my dreams, and most importantly, my ride or die partner in life. Here's the spoiler – I adore Chance Edric and we do end up happily ever after with no messy divorce fueled by high priced attorneys as we will our children to secretly despise the other one while smiling and offering words of acceptance. I am beyond lucky to be an observer and participant in his collection of ordinary and extraordinary moments. But, these three moments actually helped to shape who we are together. They are both entertaining and pivotal. Chance and I often reminisce about the first two with an air of maturity and an, "oh my frickin gawd, can you believe that happened? Ha. Ha. Ha." The third incident we don't speak about often. We know it happened. It remains a silent reminder for me as to what happens when the stresses of the outside world work their way into a relationship. It was the only time I actually saw a glimpse of what life without Chance would be – and it terrified me.

I had just turned twenty-three, married for a mere six months, and was away from my family for the very first time at Christmas. Chance and I trekked with our two cats in our Acura Integra through the snow of two northwestern states to spend Christmas with his family. My inlaws are wonderful people and have never been anything but loving, welcoming, and accepting. Still though, I was quite anxious about spending the holiday without my mom and dad. Chance was great – very attentive and understanding. We spent the couple of days before Christmas visiting friends, checking out our favorite college haunts, and eating our way through our favorite restaurants.

The morning of December 24, we woke up and I planned for another day of hanging out and doing some last-minute Christmas shopping. However, after breakfast Chance told me that he had a Christmas tradition with his friends. They all spent the day at the mall shopping – just the boys. I told him to have fun and that I would spend the day with his mom helping her to get ready for the big Christmas Eve party they hosted every year. Chance gave me a kiss, told me he'd be back no later than 5:00 PM, and headed out. My mother-in-law and I had a lovely day of baking and drinking wine.

About 5:00 PM, I went upstairs to change and get ready for a festive evening. I was actually feeling very relaxed and I was excited to spend it with my new family. At about 5:30 PM, I noticed Chance still hadn't arrived. It was snowing and my in-laws lived way up at the top of a hill so I really didn't think much of it. My sister-in-law and her family arrived as well as some family friends. We were all visiting and every once in a while, someone would ask about Chance. I brushed off the questions and said he was on his way. This was 1998 – we had no cell phones.

By 7:00 PM, it was time to eat. So, we ate without Chance.

By 8:00 PM, the house was packed with mostly people I did not know. Chance's mom and sisters were furious and did everything to keep me included and comfortable. I'm sure they could tell I was on the verge of tears. Where the hell was my husband??!! We took family pictures. I was in all the photos alone. No sign of Chance.

By 10:00 PM, I had gone past sadness. I was pissed. Meanwhile, Chance's wonderful, feisty sisters were telling me they were going to kick his ass and that I should totally leave him. They've always been my champions!

At 11:00 PM, Chance and his best friend finally graced us all with their presence. The beautiful thing was that I did not have to say one word. His own family jumped on him. When he had been sufficiently reprimanded, he returned emphatically to doting husband and did not leave my side for the rest of the trip. I credit his family completely for the continuation of our very new marriage. What he did that day is his own story to tell. I do believe this was the point when he realized that this marriage thing was a thing we had to do together and doing what he wanted when he wanted was no longer part of his agenda. Oh, and when we go to back to his hometown for Christmas now – we go to the mall together on Christmas Eve.

We were twenty-nine, we had just moved to Denver, and we were having a blast. We did not yet have children and were free to do what we wanted when we wanted. My sister and her boyfriend had also just moved to town and together with our collective college friends we were living the life. We spent weekends in downtown Denver eating, drinking, and dancing in the trendiest spots.

Halloween night was a big night out. We dressed in costumes and gathered for a night on the town. Very responsibly, we piled in taxis (no Uber yet) and headed to Market Street. We spent hours drinking and dancing.

All was well until my sister's boyfriend, Ronny, decided to stand at the doorway of an upstairs bar pretending to be a bouncer and denying entrance to some bar goers. Needless to say, he was quickly asked to leave. So we all trudged back out into the street to find another place to celebrate. Someone suggested a big warehouse dance club.

The dance club was located a couple of streets over and definitely had a shadier clientele. But it was late and we were all in high spirits, so against better judgment we all eagerly agreed to go.

The club was huge and absolutely overflowing with some scary people. Somehow, we all got separated. I was with the girls and Chance and Ronny were together. Once inside, it was dark and pulsing with electronic music. You could not hear a thing over the music. The girls left to go to the bathroom and I stayed behind to wait for Chance who still had not materialized. I went up to a balcony so I could have a better view. Chance apparently made his way through the crowd being pushed and shouted at the entire time. He was definitely intoxicated and getting upset because of the hostile environment. When he saw me standing there, he lost his mind. Chance is a very passionate, loyal person. However, jealously is something he struggled with a lot, especially in our early years. I have no idea what was going on in his head, but I was having none of it. He went into a screaming rage.

I was so furious that he was so ridiculous, I immediately left the club. I walked straight out the door and into a cab. One hundred dollars later I was home in suburban Denver. I walked upstairs and immediately heard a car door shut and then the front door open. Chance had spent an additional hundred dollars to take a cab home. I refused to speak to him and went to bed. I could hear him wrestling around in the closet. He pulled out a huge suitcase and was throwing clothes into it. I asked him what he was doing. He screamed, "I'm going to Miami!" I said ok, and climbed into bed. The next morning, I walked into the closet and he was literally sleeping in the suitcase with his cat curled up next to him. I asked if he was still planning on going to Miami. He said, "No. Do you want to go get some breakfast?" No one left for Miami and Chance doesn't drink whiskey anymore.

We had everything going for us. We had the jobs, we had the house, we had the cars, and most importantly, we had the baby we'd waited years for. But what nobody saw and nobody knew, was that our lives were crumbling.

I had a full-time job I loved that was incredibly consuming. I had a baby I had waited my entire life for who had colic, didn't sleep, and was agitated by everything. He would never let me put him down and was having a lot of difficulties at daycare that I had to hear about every day when I dropped him off and picked him up. I hadn't slept more than three hours in a row in eighteen months. I felt like an utter failure as a mother. I was overcome with guilt for putting him in daycare while I worked, but not working was financially impossible for us. I never saw my husband and when I did, he didn't want to hear about any of it and really wanted no conversation with me of any kind. I was also failing as a wife and I had no one to confide in.

Chance worked for one of the big banks. It was a demanding job that consisted of working during the day and entertaining clients at night. Whenever I asked about what he was doing or where he was going, I got nothing but irritation from him. When he wasn't working, he was going out with friends.

Our lives had been completely turned upside down with the arrival of our son. I could no longer go out with Chance. I was very jealous of Chance's freedom and I don't think he understood how completely isolated I felt.

We were both mad. I cried. He yelled. It was terrible. We simply were unable to see the other's frustration with the situation. We both felt as though we were the victim. One night he told me to leave the baby upstairs and come down and talk with him. He said the words. "I can't do this anymore." I said fine and walked away.

We both immediately realized the weight of what that meant. We both started crying. He apologized and I apologized and we made a plan. For the first time in a long time, we actually listened to each other. We vowed to make it work.

In the following six months we sold the house and moved in order to push the reset button. We began parenting together and made an effort to go out together at least twice a month without the baby. It worked. We were connecting again and loving our unit of three. We actually were doing so well that we got a very big surprise – baby number two! Unplanned and unexpected, but greatly anticipated.

Whenever we have our moments now, I simply go back to that time and remember. I remember what could have happened and I forgive, understand, and listen. Chance has grown into the most amazing father. He loves his children more than anything and they absolutely adore him. His weekends are spent with us and I believe he loves it. I also know that he loves me and that this is my real thing.

"Somebody's knocking, should I let him in? Lord it's the devil, would you look at him." —Terri Gibbs

Chapter 18

Laughter From Beyond

My daughter and son-in-law, Chance, aren't the only ones who have experienced strange brushes with the supernatural. The ways of the past seem to always catch up with the ways of the present. Here are some accounts of my past that helped me see the world in a whole different light, or darkness, as it may be.

My mother was a God-fearing Wisconsin Synod Lutheran. The strictest Lutheran church – Catholic in every sense of the word except that we didn't believe in the Pope and we believed in the devil with a vengeance.

Strict rules governed our house: no cussing (not even shucks, gosh, or darn), no short skirts, no make-up, no gambling, not ever taking the name of God in vain, and absolutely no rock and roll (otherwise you would go straight to hell). A curious rule was no board games, except Going to Jerusalem which consisted of the twelve disciples, each being eight inches tall, wending their way to the holy city at the mercy of the roll of dice. And...the Ouija board. No kidding; I don't know if mama wasn't aware of the nature of the game or she thought it an intriguing way to outsmart the old devil.

Part of her thinking could have been her weird fascination with the occult. Back in Wisconsin where she grew up, they had table rise parties. Four or more young couples would get together regularly to gather around a table, place their fingertips lightly on the table in front of them, and join their thumbs together. They then would hook pinkies with the person next to them so that there was an unbroken chain around the table. They would all close their eyes and "concentrate". One person would firmly ask a yes or no question. They would all breathlessly wait for the "answer". The table would rise up on three legs and slowly tap down on the fourth leg – once for yes, twice for no. Very eerie and freaky. We kids witnessed this many times. Truly – it worked and no trickery involved. We spent hours with the Ouija board. We asked it everything and believed in it with all our hearts. This went on for several years. Our questions got creepier and creepier as we got older, and some weird stuff began happening to our family.

My parents would go out for the evening and leave the three of us home alone. We lived five miles from town in an old farmhouse with two stories and a full basement. Our nearest neighbors were two miles down the road. Once the car drove out of the driveway, the groaning and moaning would begin. The furnace was a huge monster that ate oil; it would shudder to a halt and in order to restart it, one of us would have to go into the basement to the far back room where it lived and tip the glass tube to click the beast back on. We would sit in the cold as long as we could stand it, then draw straws to see which poor chump had to venture down into the bowels of the house. The unlucky individual would slink down, tiptoe to the massive door, push it open, and dash to the glass cylinder located up so high we could barely reach it – *stretching* up on our toes to give it a tap. The roaring would start and we knew we were doomed. Truly something was chasing us all the way back upstairs. You'd almost pass out from fear and we always had a sick, airless feeling by the time we returned. The house seemed to be in pain and we as little kids didn't have the words to describe this phenomenon to our parents. "Stop being such sissies" was the comment we got from dear old dad. Mom would tell us to ask Jesus to take care of us.

One summer afternoon, my sister, brother, and I were sitting on the couch in the living room. Suddenly the sky turned dark, almost black, and a ferocious wind came up. Thunder began booming, almost deafening; very unusual in Wyoming where we lived on the red desert. My siblings and I looked at each other, "what the fuck!!" Suddenly the screen door flew open and a ball of fire flew in the house! It seemed to be the size of a bowling ball and flames were licking all around the edges. It came straight at us and we ducked. The ball swerved and headed for the kitchen trailing flicks of fire. Meanwhile, to quote Garth Brooks, "...and the thunder rolled". The fire ball flew hell bent for leather out the kitchen window. The three of us stared after it and simultaneously began screaming at the top of our lungs. We jumped off the couch and ran for the basement: there sat the Ouija board atop the pool table where we had left it the previous night.

One Saturday, my little brother and I were rambling around looking for something to do. We were experts at "running the rails" on the top of the corrals. We were always barefoot in the summer, and were able to grab the wood with our little toes. My little brother loved fire and was always looking for some extra excitement. We were trotting around the tops of the cow pens when suddenly my brother decided to check out his pockets. Sure enough there was a match! As we ran, he flicked the match with his thumb nail and tossed it into the corral. POOF!! Fire like we'd never seen, snaking along the ground toward all that wood. Down we jumped to grab the hose. No way were we getting any grown-up help, we'd be murdered! Spraying the fire just seemed to feed it as it grew and grew. Our only hope was mom, who immediately called the fire department. The trucks came tearing down the road full throttle and sirens wailing. Unfortunately, they had to drive right in front of my dad's construction company on their way out of town. Big bad dad jumped into his Cadillac and followed them out. Good God, it took forever to douse the fire! The manure smoked for days and the firemen said, "pretty weird how that little match done all this". We knew deep down what the real cause was: Ouija board Juju again.

During this same period of time the family fell on hard times: my sister became a tortured soul and fell into heavy drug and alcohol abuse. She spent hours separating out the orange grains from Contac pills so she could get a big bunch to gulp all at once. She was in lala land for hours afterward. My dad's drinking escalated and my mom turned to Valium and booze. My little brother started disappearing for days at a time only to eventually resurface and looking like a ghost. "I've been over at Jim's" was a typical explanation. When my brother burned the dog house down in a terrifying burst of flames, my dear mama was through with it all.

I don't know if it was a revelation or act of desperation, but one day I got off the school bus and found her out back by the old bunkhouse. She had a roaring bonfire going and on top of it was the Ouija board. She was sending it back to the devil.

"Wooo hooo witchy woman see how high she flies" — Eagles

Chapter 19

The Seers

Since the dawn of time, there have been so many false prophets. There have also been so many documented occurrences of unexplainable phenomenon, and so many signs in the midst of reality. I never thought that this would be the footnote in a rather exquisite world. I truly believe that nothing truly ends. Energy is forever. Even when it's negative energy. It's still a force. It's still all around, whether we acknowledge it or not.

I'm writing this last because it seems to go along so perfectly with the rest of this book, but I know that my story isn't done yet. The best I can do is offer my own point of view in these last few words. Take it all how you will. In the end, I think that whatever higher power there is will make the final call. Probably. I'm not here to tell you what to think.

These last few stories are my own accounts and happenings with the people who can see beyond, or whatever you want to call it. I'm not a superstitious guy, but I can't help but acknowledge there are people that are in the know. And, for whatever reason, they are able to communicate with whatever energy is out there.

Let me start with this. In my experience, psychics, seers, clairvoyants, and witches are about ninety-nine percent bullshit.

Why so high?

Well, honestly, I blame the internet. The profound amount of information you can find out about someone with Google and a few other quick tools is actually quite scary. People want to believe. The internet, mixed with a little pop psychology, is usually enough to convince them that they are the real deal. Even when they aren't.

If you really want to dive down a rabbit hole, try reading any forum by the ones that will admit to it. You might be surprised at how many will admit to leading people down bogus pathways that in the end only result in profit for themselves. Sometimes, there are entire companies built around the "business." It's astounding.

So when I tell you about my stories, I'm not just feeding you a line about how you should go to your nearest fortune teller and get a nice fortune. I'm going out on a limb and telling you about the few times I have actually run into something different.

"Went to the fortune teller to have my fortune read" — The Rolling Stones

Chapter 20

Proceed with Extreme Caution

The first time I met someone with capabilities to see beyond, it was at a millionaire's birthday party. Someone hired a psychic to cater to the rich guests and give them all a glimpse into their futures. The ultimate hand job.

She rolled up in the stereotypical theatrical outfit. There was a feather hat that lead to her feathered boa. Do you remember Tom Hanks' movie, *Big*? She looked like that toy gypsy gal in the fortune telling machine. Except alive. She waltzed right over to me.

"May I give you a reading?" She asked me. I was a little startled at her directness. My wife and my friends looked over with wonder and amusement.

"Sure," I said, "What could it hurt?"

If there's one thing I've learned about fortune tellers and really about any advice givers in general, it's that their words aren't going to hurt. If they say something bad is coming, take it as a chance to be more cautious. If it sounds good, then feel good about things. Their words aren't going to change things. *You* are. If someone wants to tell you things are going well and send some love your way, take that positive energy and run with it. Just remember, it's *you* that will end up living your life.

The gypsy teller asked everyone else to leave. She needed to concentrate and didn't want to be tainted by everyone else's reactions. She told me to sit down and that her name was Anne. I hadn't really said anything, or done anything remarkable when she asked me, "What do you want to know?"

I'm sure my eyes went wide as I said, "Uh... I have no idea. You are the first psychic I've ever talked to."

"Ahhh," she cooed, "A virgin. We love those."

I had to stop myself from rolling my eyes. Of course a psychic would love fresh meat. You could con them from the start and they'd never even see it coming.

She then pulled out a stack of tarot cards from a pocket in her dress.

"Let us just see what the forces around you are saying," she said.

"Sure," I told her, again trying not to be rude but not buying into it.

With appropriate dramatic flair, she fanned out her tarot cards and started to pull them out and lay them down. I couldn't tell you which ones she pulled out or what exactly they were supposed to mean.

Unfortunately, it seemed like she knew little more than I did about them. She gave me some vague "prophecies" of my future and what had happened before in my life. Nothing there was earth-shattering or even particularly out of the ordinary. She told me in a vague way that things were going to be good, and that I would have a long, successful life. There were some "anger points" to be dealt with. You know, the kind of things that are common to all of the human family.

In other words, complete bullshit. Call it confirmation bias, but it was exactly what I expected.

When I got back to the group, they asked me how it went. I gave them a three second synopsis and we all had a good laugh. It didn't cost more than a small tip, so I didn't mind too much. Even if it was a con, I don't mind someone helping me believe in a positive future.

I've paid people more and gotten treated way worse.

"We're up all night to get lucky." —Daft Punk

Chapter 21

What Gets Spent in Vegas

It was a warm June day and I was sitting at the Las Vegas airport waiting with the untold thousands to get on my plane headed home. The week had been a successful trip to my regional office. I had some fun, and made some solid relationships on the work front. As always, Vegas had left me tired and a little lighter in the wallet.

As I was checking my email, I noticed a few people around me were grumbling under their breath and pointing towards our plane entrance gate. I turned to see what they were all looking at when a TV caught my eye. It was actually showing pictures of the airport I was flying home to, Denver International Airport. At the bottom of the screen a banner read, "DIA shut down for first time due to wind."

So I wasn't going home? I sulked over to the ticket agent who confirmed it with a tired smile. Denver International Airport was shutting down ninety percent of the runways because the cross wind was so strong they could not land the planes safely. They had cancelled all flights for the night, but I could always stick around in case the weather changed. There was also the slight possibility that I could get on one of those few planes that might be able to land on the one runway open. By now it was 6:30 PM, and the idea of sitting at an airport wasn't my idea of a good time.

Here's the thing. If you have no control over getting back home, don't sweat it. Unless you have a major emergency (i.e. your baby is due, it's your wife's or kid's birthday, etc.), do yourself the favor and stay the extra night. Especially if you are on the company's time and dollar. If there's nothing you can do about it, don't get mad. Look at it as an extended adventure. At least that's the way I always tried taking those very rare times I was stuck somewhere.

So after a quick call to my boss, my supervisor, and the wife, I was cleared of any issues surrounding me being stuck another day in Vegas. Now, it was time to call my hotel and get a room for the night.

I usually stay at the Palms when I go to Vegas, whether for work or play, so I had an account there and had just stayed two nights prior.

However, when I got to the VIP host they informed me they were booked solid because of some events going on in the hotel that night. Using a little charm and some customer appreciation I was able to get them to not only find me a room, but for the same price I always pay they got me a suite in the newest tower they just completed.

Sweet. Now I had a nice room in a hotel where something important was going on. It was time to find out what could book up the Palms on a Sunday night.

In the four hours I had been at the airport, the Palms had completely changed. Mobile lights were now set up around the main entrance. In the parking lot was a sea of news vans. It wasn't just the local ones either. I noticed Entertainment Tonight fighting for a good spot near the front.

I figured it meant there was some celebrity stuff. Cool.

The crowd was already assembled when I got to the door, and everyone was dressed to the nines. I'll tell you that I didn't feel quite dressed up enough downstairs, but when I got up to the last-minute luxury suite they had to switch me to I didn't mind one bit.

I walked downstairs to the center bar to finally figure out what was going on. As I sat there, ordering some food, a younger gentleman and his *very* dressed up date sat down next to me.

"Do you know what all the hubbub is about?" I asked, trying not to interrupt.

"Yeah, man," he said. "It's a double feature tonight. We're here for the Ozomatli concert."

"The Oz what?" I asked, in total ignorance.

"Ozomatli," he repeated. "Yeah, man, they're huge in Mexico. They're like the Grateful Dead of Mexico. Cult Latino following that sells out all of their shows no matter where they go. They're awesome, man."

"Huh," was all I could think of to say. I had never heard anything about them.

"There's also a movie premier. Ocean's 13. You know, man, Clooney, Pacino, Robert, Damon, Cheadle, and the works are at a new theatre here at the Palms. Rumor says they're trying to do a film fest here."

I'm not much of a groupie or a celeb lover in general, but tonight, you could feel the energy in this place. There was a lot happening and it was just fun to be a part of it.

Later that night, I stood outside to watch for the celebs, just to see them. If I cared enough, I probably could have fought through the ten rows of people to get to the front and try to touch the stars. But to me, it really wasn't worth the effort. I could see well enough from the back.

I will say that it was impressive to see that many of the A-list stars out, walking the red carpet. They looked great and were cordial to their fans, saying hi to random people. Then they went inside to their premier.

I, on the other hand, was starting to feel that Las Vegas itch again. I wanted to gamble.

The floor of the casino was packed. Every table was packed. Everyone was pushing up the bets, trying to win big. The lowest tables were starting at twenty-five dollars, and I wasn't quite ready to spend that kind of money on a single game.

I saw something out of the corner of my eye. Back then, the Palms had a whole bunch of shops around the perimeter of the card tables. There were ink tattoo parlors, boutiques, and gift shops. And then, in one tucked away, dark little corner, there was a darkened plate glass window with a warm red glow emitting from it.

I was curious, and that light pulled on my curiosity like a moth to a flame.

As soon as I walked past the black, velvet drapes, I saw exactly what I suspected might be in that corner shop. Have you ever seen the movie *Aladdin*, with Robin Williams? In the beginning of that movie there is a fortune teller with all the stereotypical traits of what you think a fortune teller would look like. I could have sworn that this place was dedicated to his memory. The only difference between the lady in this shop and the teller from the movie was the lack of a beard. On the table, she had a crystal ball that she kept her hand poised over, like it was going to reveal the mysteries of the universe to her.

I had already had my first experience with a psychic and figured, why not sit down and pay a stranger to chat? That's what you do when you buy someone a beer in a bar, right?

"Hello, and thank you for visiting Miss Felicity's curiosity shop," she said in a perfectly-practiced, raspy witch voice. I hid a smile. This was going to be fun, I thought. Let's play.

We started to tango. She started out simply asking what I wanted to know from her. From my first encounter, I had a little bit of an idea of what to ask. I also wanted to see what I could do to throw her off. I wanted to see how "real" she could get.

"Nothing," I said, flatly. "I just want to see what you see in my presence."

"Perfect," she said, keeping a straight face. "I knew you were coming, anyway." Again I worked to keep a straight face. This girl was a little different from the last. She was younger and didn't have any tarot cards that I could see. She did have that big crystal ball in the center of the table though, looking very much like a movie prop. She looked me up and down with her intense eyes and smiled a weird, knowing smile that she had probably perfected in the mirror with her voice.

"You have a very beautiful soul. The aura or light emitting from your being is such a bright blue and deep green. No shades of red, no dark edges. You are a very lucky person and have been very successful in all your endeavors so far," she rasped.

Great, I thought, here we go with the super generic statements. And how nice of her to say such positive vagaries.

To be fair, I usually try to dress a little better than most my age, and I always have an air of confidence about me. So it's no surprise that the ultimate con job could figure those out.

She must have sensed my apprehension or saw the incredulous look in my eyes, because she suddenly reached across the table and grabbed my hand.

"I get it. I have been doing this long enough to see the rolling eyes, the snickering after someone leaves. I understand. I didn't want this gift I have. I was given it and try to use it to help people. But here is the thing. Whatever compelled you to come in here, it's just as compelling to me. You have an incredible strong force around you. You are extremely protected and blessed. You always will be. Much more so than most of the people that have walked through my door." Again, such great compliments.

"No offense to you or anyone that does your job," I told her, "but I have limited experience with people who claim to have otherworldly sight. I have tried and tried to sense the other side. I have done things that most people would not dare to do to see some sort of proof. And every time I've tried, I get nothing."

I would eventually find evidence of something bigger out there, which you have already read, but at this point in my life, I was still skeptical.

"I'm really just interested in the other side or whatever else might be out there. You are correct. I have been in multiple situations that I probably shouldn't have survived. There are reasons why I shouldn't be here in front of you. Quite honestly, there are times I wonder if I shouldn't be on the other side of whatever might be out there. That said, if you've got something specific, I sure would like hear about it."

She looked over me with renewed interest. "Yeah, you are a smart one. You can take a lot of the things that are around you and see them at different values and different options to you. You would be surprised at how many people out there are not able to do that. I feel sorry for them. So you want me to see your love life? Your financial life? Your longevity? No problem. Fair warning to you though. I do not hold anything back. If it's good I will tell you. If it's bad, I will tell you. I do not manipulate the future, I simply let people know what I am told."

I wasn't sure I could ask for much more. Intrigued, I relaxed back in my chair and let her do her thing.

"You have a very, very healthy love life. I see many years with the same person. I also do not feel many struggles in your love life, but there is strife coming. Nothing that looks or feels detrimental. Just some very large bumps that could deter and test that relationship. Do not stray too far from that though. It's what has been grounding you to this point and will do so for the rest of your life if you let it. Which I see happening, but there will be choices. You will be very successful in the not too far, but further future. Whatever it is that you are doing now will serve its need to further you to that point. You are destined along your current work path but I see even that deviating in the near future.

Something more you will feel at ease with. I also see you beginning to accept and open your third eye. Seeing things in an even different way."

I had no idea what a third eye even was. I was hoping that it didn't have to do with my nether regions. She continued, "I see you and your significant other living a very long and healthy life and your children and their children around you. Oh, and I am getting a sign or a low voice that's wanting me to tell you that it's ok. Even at the points later in life when you feel exasperated, or when you feel the world has piled everything on top of you, that it's ok. It's all part of the plan and the pieces of the puzzle sometimes do not fit perfectly, but they all end up fitting for a reason."

With that, she lurched out of her trance, smiled at me, grabbed my hand, and then proceeded to tell me that her services will cost me sixty dollars and that there is no need for further questions.

"You are being watched and guarded by something beyond your comprehension and you also have loved ones you don't know that are around at all times, protecting you."

Your fifteen minutes are up, now pay me and get out. Biggest fucking scam ever!

I walked out feeling like I had gotten nothing more than the last woman. It was all positive, telling me that there would be bumps and hard times but that it would all be fine. With that sixty bucks I could have won better advice at the tables. Lucy gave Charlie Brown the same advice and she only charged five cents. Maybe feeling stupid was one of those "bumps" that was coming.

The only weird thing that happened was when I stumbled upon the club where the Ocean's 13 stars were partying. I was sitting at the bar, watching random women trying to sneak into the VIP sections to schmooze with Clooney and Damon when I felt a hand on my shoulder.

When I turned around, there was a very beautiful woman. I was apologizing for standing too close to their VIP table when she looked me over and said, "Has anyone ever told you that you have an incredible aura about you? Your whole essence is bright, bright, and bright!" Then she smiled and walked over to George Clooney, who gave her a quick hug and a kiss.

I guess even a broken clock is right twice a day.

"Down in Louisiana, where the black trees grow, lives a voodoo lady named Marie Laveau" —Bobby Bare

Chapter 22

I Met a Ghost

It was a crisp October afternoon when I got off the plane in New Orleans for my first trip into the city of magic, gumbo, and the dead. My wife let me plan an impromptu trip with one of my coworkers and I was lucky to find a way to make it somewhat work related, even though the trip was all play and very little work.

My coworker, Bill, had convinced me after a trip to see Pearl Jam in my hometown that he wanted me and a couple other friends to go to New Orleans and see the Voodoo fest where Pearl Jam was headlining. It took some negotiating, but I worked it out and was looking forward to a great time.

After picking up my baggage, I gave Bill a call. He told me they had just pulled into the RV Park where we were going to be staying. Bill had taken an eight-hour road trip in his father's huge RV, all the way from Dallas, with two other good friends. We were all going to stay in that park, so I caught a cab and headed over towards RV heaven.

If you've never been there, New Orleans strikes you first as being a really old city. You can sense the loss and hurt it's suffered, even as recently as Hurricane Katrina. But, even with all that, the city has a sense of culture and creativity that you just can't ignore. It is part art, part booze, and all party.

My cabbie and I had a conversation as we drove through the city, and he told me about its history. He told me about the do's and don'ts of the town and the districts to avoid. I caught a bit of hesitation in his voice when he mentioned the district I was going to as one of the darker ones. I wish I had known beforehand, but it was a little late now. If nothing else, it was close to the park where the festival was.

Finally, the taxi dropped me off in front of the twenty-foot walls of the RV Park. I looked at the razor wire on the top, distractedly paying the cabbie. As soon as my tip was through the window though, I heard his rubber burning as he pealed out of the neighborhood. It didn't make me feel good, especially because it was barely 3:00 PM.

When I found the RV, Bill had driven down for us, I had to admit that it was very nice. It was nicer than any RV I had ever stayed in. The only problem was that it looked tiny compared with some of the other ones in the park.

A lot of the bands that were going to play in the festival were staying there as well. Big names like Trent Reznor from Nine Inch Nails, and Kid Rock and his crew. The guys from The Cure were there, too. I'm not sure how Bill managed to find this place, but it was awesome.

We were all newbies to New Orleans, so naturally we wanted to taste and try out all the touristy crap that the locals hate. We wandered the city, calling it N'awlins as if we were natives, and playing up our part as tourists. One of the oldest graveyards recorded in America happened to be outside the east wall of where our RV was. It's called St. Louis Cemetery No.1, and it houses the grave of Marie Laveau, the Voodoo Queen of New Orleans. That tombstone was literally across the wall from us. It was a fun start to the weekend.

New Orleans was fun. Everyone was just getting along and doing whatever we wanted. It was definitely a dark city. Many, many sins are evident and almost out in the open. We learned quickly that in a city like that, you need to know what you're getting into and stay within the confines of your comforts. There weren't any fights, or anything really creepy. Just amazing music, great vibes, and a very chill history lesson.

We were in the French Quarter the last couple of days, and had spent enough time there to get our bearings. By that point, we were ready for something more on the outskirts of tourist central. We wanted to check out some of the darker side of the magic that is New Orleans. For that, we headed to one of the oldest Voodoo shops in town.

We got there and found it was everything we wanted and then some. The service was rude, and heavy incense covered a lingering smell of death. Every tchotchke, toy, or product that you never thought you wanted was there, including more than a few things that you legitimately couldn't find anywhere else. Where else do you buy dried bird heads?

Sitting on top of some old parchment books on a counter there was also a clipboard. I took a quick glance and realized that it was a sign up for their in-house fortune teller. I asked the girl behind the register about it. She mentioned it was seventy-five dollars, and while this one in particular was always booked, there were two spots open if we could wait around for forty minutes.

My buddy's wife was very into it, and I was always on the lookout for the real deal. I had to tell her of my two previous experiences. Undeterred she said, "So if I go in and do it, will you go after me?" Psychics have always intrigued me, and I want to believe. I'm also skeptical, and wonder if it's all a scam.

In the end, I agreed. We had plenty of time. Everyone was entertained and they sold beer right next door, so why not?

Thirty minutes later, my buddie's wife went first. A little less than an hour, she came to get me.

"How was it?" I asked.

Her face was a little white, but she smiled nervously and said, "It was awesome. I can't believe the things she knew. There is no way...no way... and all of it wasn't good. I don't know. It was awesome. But scary."

Intrigued to say the least, I was also wary of what I knew I had already signed up for. I figured that of course, some of the con artists must be better at their job than others. Even so, I couldn't help but wonder. She seemed genuinely happy *and* scared. It was an interesting mix.

As I sat in the small waiting room, I couldn't help but notice it was void of anything significant. There were no turbans, crystal balls, or tarot cards. Nothing. Just a round table with a plain white cloth draped over it and a couple of chairs. One window let in a sliver of sunlight from the alleyway.

Seventy-five dollars for this? I thought. I better get an hour at least out of it.

Then, after a few minutes, the seer walked in. My jaw dropped as she sat down and she said in a sweet, hushed voice, "Did you see a ghost?"

I thought I did.

The woman who walked in was a little old lady, about four foot nine. She must have been in her late sixties, or maybe early seventies. But what really got me was her face.

Between her haircut, her glasses, and the way she walked into the room, it was like my own mother had just walked through the door. I kept checking to make sure that it *wasn't* her.

"First off," I said, "I have to tell you why I may have seemed startled when you first walked in. Not sure if you noticed or not. But when you came in I swore that I was seeing my mom here as a joke. I can clearly now see and tell you are not my mother, but it was interesting since I wasn't expecting to see her here," I said with nervous hesitation.

She laughed, just like my mom, and told me that she was mostly certain that she wasn't my mom. Then she looked at me conspiratorially and said, "But I'm not one hundred percent sure."

I slowly shook myself out of it, and she came forward to take my hands.

"What is it that I can offer you?" she asked. "Why were you drawn to come here and seek my advice?"

"To answer your question, I really do not have anything specific. Let us just see where our conversation goes and if you feel you need to tell me anything." I said with an uneven tone and lower register in my voice.

Of course, I thought uncertainly, the long con begins. I wasn't sure if they had dressed her up purposely as my mom, but I wasn't about to give in that easily. I only gave my first name. I even switched my wedding ring to a different finger. Anything to try to throw off my "tell" signs.

"Well, that does explain some things for sure," She cooed in a grandmotherly southern drawl. "You look like a sweet young man and I see a lot of positive things around you and in your near future."

She then grabbed onto my hand tighter.

"But, I have to tell you something very important. In the very near future, I am seeing five or six months, you are going to have a big shake up with your current employer. Please, do not fear what comes down the road after that. The path you will be led upon is not going to be easy, but I promise you that it's all set and you will move on to better things. Things that you are meant for. Does any of that make any sense at all?"

I smiled, more on the inside than the outside. I was with a co-worker of mine that worked directly with me. I had changed sales territories and while I wasn't blowing up their records, I was doing well enough and besides, it was a tough sales territory for what I did.

However, being a new dad to my son, I was stressed to the core. Then there was the fact that I was about to be an even newer dad. My job had long hours and a lot of expectations. But even with all that, my life was still relatively smooth sailing. Strike one for my mom's stunt double.

"Well, that's interesting," I replied. "I will be on the watch for anything down the road. So far all is well. I've been with my company for years, and don't see change on the horizon. But, thank you." It's always good to be polite to your mom, no matter the situation.

She let go of my hand. "I do not mean to frighten you. I only want to share what I see around you and for you in your future. Everything is good, Chance. You have had some recent struggles and some more serious struggles are coming up, in all different facets of your life. Professional. Personal. Life in general. I want you to know there is so much good for you coming past those momentary struggles. For you, your spouse, and your children."

My brain's incessant skeptical whining all froze at that exact moment. I hadn't told her I was married. My ring was on the other finger. I took multiple steps to make "reading" things about me harder.

Wait, my brain thought as it slowly worked through the problem. I've been married for years, so there's ring wear on my ring finger. Damn; she's good, but still no cigar.

But children? I only had my three-year-old son at that point. Our daughter was a huge, wonderful surprise but generally unknown. We had only told a few people so far, and didn't want to jinx anything. With the issues we'd had with our son, we just wanted to make sure. Also, we had barely learned we were having a daughter less than a week before. Almost no one knew that. Not even many of my friends and immediate family. And, she said children…

"Let me tell you something," she resumed as my brain continued to process. "Both of your children are blessed. They are definitely here, and coming for reasons beyond your comprehension, for now. Your little daughter who is on the way, she is an absolute ball of energy. Good energy. Vivid energy. She is going to come blasting into this world and take charge and never back down. She is going to be very holy, I think. I don't necessarily see holiness like a nun, or clergy, but there is utter goodness attached to her. She is destined to help many people in some way or some form. She is also going to be dramatic."

"Oh wait, I see you rolling your eyes. Yes. Women are dramatic. I do not mean that way. I see her in a very dramatic role for her life like an actress, or a musician. It'll be something very creative that needs that level of drama. I don't know. She is so bright. So loving. I think that's where the holiness I feel around her comes from. You are already a very lucky person. I sense that from you. But she is an absolute lucky charm. An absolute gem!" She stopped to let it soak in.

And, soak in it did. Did I really just hear all that? I had so many questions. My brain was flying, trying to figure out what technology she and the store used to gain that info. Was there a chip reader under the table getting my credit card info and cross checking it with purchases? I can understand them finding me on Facebook and gleaning some info off that. But how did she know about my unborn daughter? Especially when so many people close to me didn't know, let alone the world.

Still smiling but caught off guard, I said, "I like all this positive love I am getting! I have no idea how you knew about my daughter or some of those other things, but it sounds like I will have my hands full for sure. Thank you for the generous heads up. We just found out last week we are having a girl, who was already a surprise. We haven't even broached the subject of names. We have some ideas, but for the most part we are just in the happy stage."

She smiled over at me. "You know, my grandson is an absolute ball. He's all of two-years old and is just a shining beam of light, for the most part. As all young children are and always will be. He is hilarious. He grew up in Maine, and has had very limited exposure to the Deep

South. But for some reason he now likes to talk with a southern accent and drawl when he gets very excited. Which is something that I know comes from a place of great intelligence."

I had no idea why she brought this up. It was so random. But then again, it wasn't.

"That is so random, but very helpful," I explained. "You see, our son, who has almost no connection with the South or its beautiful people does that, too. It's absolutely frigging hilarious. When he gets himself stuck, or he and I are play wrestling and he can't get away, he will scream, 'MAH-MAH, HELP ME! HELP ME, MAH-MAH,' in the most adorable Tennessee slow southern drawl. We have no idea where he gets it as none of the people in his life, or very little TV he watches, have this accent."

She reached over and grabbed my arm again. "I need to tell you this. That boy is so amazingly smart. I know that you and your wife have already sensed that. Please play to that. Let that little man explore to what you guys can give him and allow him to do without going over the lines. He is so full of wonderment. I know he took a lot of effort getting here. I know he has taken more time and energy than either of you have. It will get better. I promise. There is going to always be that battle with him and you. Just know it comes from a good place, even if you can't see that through some anger or pain. He is going to be something great. Something to do with building or creating. I can also see some sort of hard science in him. Nurture that. Stand firm in setting the rules, on your side. Do that and you will help him blossom to his fullest!"

She couldn't have known how true most of those statements were, could she? How could she know how much we struggled and how much we threw on the line for that little man? But we wouldn't have done it any other way. Especially now, looking back at the very near past. It's been laden with many metaphorical land mines, but we have maneuvered well enough. Tough road for sure. But life wouldn't be fun if it was all cupcakes and rainbows.

This was weird, but again, who am I to not take some positive vibes and run with it? And of course, she was saying positive things about my kids. Why wouldn't I take that? And, if I'm being honest, even if it was a long con there were some morsels in there that came from nowhere. I had only visited with three of these "seers," and didn't have a wide base of experience to compare. They were each different.

This one was radically different. Specific events and somewhat specific timing. Enough that made me jot down the info into my memory.

Our conversation gravitated towards more general conversation, as if with a close aunt. There were no specific questions, just an open conversation about the present and the future. We talked about my wife and my friends. We talked about things that were all very positive and all informational, for the future. Then I left.

Early March, the next year

My baby daughter was born. Everything was different this time compared to our son.

My wife was way less stressed this time around. There was no sickness or weird mood swings. Nothing like the struggles she went through as a first-time mother. It was even a pleasant, quick stay at the hospital.

We were in that evening, and out the next afternoon. Our son took close to twenty hours from getting to the hospital to entering this world. That little sucker wanted to stay in that protected, happy world and fought with all his might to keep from entering the real world.

Our daughter? By the time my wife was induced, I could have sworn I heard our baby daughter screaming, "Get me out! This world is mine for the taking!" My wife was in the final stages of labor for nearly eight hours with my son. Our daughter took under a minute.

I looked over as the nurse was writing on her chart and I saw my little girl's crown pop out.

"Uh, doc?" I said, "I think the baby's here?"

The nurse looked over, hit the panic button, and within thirty seconds it went from four of us in the room to close to twenty.

My little girl burst into this world with big, bright blue eyes.

We had crossed off so many names since we learned we were having a girl. When we got to the hospital we were still unsure. In fact, it was about an hour before our daughter was born that we both came up with the name we loved, was as special as she was going to be. It was a perfect fit.

You see, her brother got to be JD. JD because we both always just loved that name. Not necessarily standing for anything. Just the initials and connection. However, it did end up working out all the way around. My father's name is Jon and Ava's father's name is David. He would go by JD, but his full name is Jon David. My daughter's name had some connection too. She would be Julianna Grace. We took the Grace from my wife's recently passed grandmother.

A few days later, we were home and slowly settling in. Even our cat, Chuck Norris, who had been skittish and utterly afraid of our son, had taken to the newest little angel.

That's when I got the call that changed a lot of things in my life. In the end, it was all for good. At the time, it was so terribly timed that it was about as big of a blow as we could have experienced.

After I took my federally mandated week of paternity leave with my company, they called the day I was back and told me they were laying me off. I had thirteen years with them. Then, with a phone call and an email, I was no longer employed. They were downsizing and I was part of a voluntary reduction in force. In other words: no longer employed.

Right after I came home from one of the best days of my life, I was let go. I had a new baby girl, a three-year-old son, an amazing wife (who fortunately was steadily employed), and Chuck-friggin-Norris. It was all suddenly on the line in a very short amount of time. Then I remembered what my mom's doppelganger had told me in a small room in New Orleans almost six months ago.

Not long after, I decided to Google my daughter's name. I was directed to the Wiki page for the origin of it. That is when I got the largest smile I could remember, and world's largest crocodile tear rolling down my left cheek.

Julian was a Latin origin name that is the base of Julianna. It listed the world's most famous Julianna's. Guess what I found out a few days after my daughter was born, just hours after I found out I was no longer a provider for my family? Julian was the name of many early saints until the early 1800's. In the late 1800's to current times, each Julianna has been an actress, musician, or athlete. I can't wait to see mine grow.

"But in the end, it doesn't even matter" —Linkin Park

Chapter 23

Fortunate Wanderer

It had been close to three years since the experience in the last chapter. To my eerie surprise, things had played out just as my mother's stunt double had told me they would. Everything she had said was always in the back of my mind, and it seemed like I could watch them materialize, even waiting patiently for the ones that took more time. I found that I could put a lot of problems on the back burner, and was better for it. Not that I was ever horrible, mind you, but I definitely lost my way for a little there. Kind of a... one-third... life crisis? Sure. We'll go with that.

Things had changed. My job was all I had ever wanted, and then some. It felt like I was finally getting to that rosy part of life that all three psychics had been predicting for me. Don't get me wrong. It wasn't everything they had said, nor had they been horribly specific, but it sure was close to what they all three had predicted.

My relationship with my wife and kids had settled down and was in an overall great place. There were bumps like there always are, and we were not perfect. But then, no one ever is. What I could say was that overall, everything was getting better by the day. A lot of that had to do with my change in attitude as well as some other environmental coincidences that seemed to be guiding me to what the three ladies had seen.

There were days in the very recent past that I literally had to pinch myself.

Despite all the trouble and confusion I had caused or been a part of in my life, I was happy. I had the perfect little family, awesome friends, and no major drama. There had always been drama, and I was usually a catalyst for it.

I think that when I get complacent, or bored, it's just a natural reaction for my soul to start to itch, looking for something. I've got Native American ancestry, and sometimes I think I really should have gone out on a walkabout and looked for the *signs* to help direct me. Then I remember I'm in the corporate world and I have responsibilities to provide for my family. I'm not sure that a week of peyote would go over very well. Besides, as you may have deduced alcohol, for all its terrible attributes, has been my drug of choice. Luckily, my kids have helped slow that down.

It was an oddly beautiful day in the early fall in Colorado, and everything was going so well. Maybe the simple peace of it all was why I felt an odd tinge in my soul. It was a feeling of unease, like there was just something not right in the universe.

I knew the feeling. My thoughts and my inner self were clogged up. I just felt like I needed something more out of life. It was within my reach but I couldn't see it. This doesn't happen often to me. I got that feeling a little more at my prior job, but I could usually get it figured out on my own. This time around though I felt my body out of whack, my mind out of whack, and like I needed some sort of direction in general. I was blocked.

I didn't even know where to go. The closest I had ever come to seeing a seer in Colorado was up in Estes Park. But that involved trying to get an appointment and a lot of hassle in a faraway, if beautiful, land.

No, what I needed was to find something local, near my work that day. I was headed up to Wheat Ridge and Golden to finish up some business, and figured maybe I could find something up there.

There's always been something about Golden. It's not just the Coors Factory. Maybe it's because it was the first place we went house hunting in Colorado, before settling in downtown Denver.

In fact, the whole reason we decided to move to Colorado had to do with an experience we had after parking downtown in Denver to explore. After parking for our very first tour of Denver, we got out of the car and approached a weird yellow burlap sack over the top of the parking meters. Now, we had just come from California and were very used to paying for parking, so we lifted the bag and started searching our pockets for quarters to put in the machine. From across the street, probably a block and a half away, we heard a funny yell.

"*Stop!!*" a woman was screaming, running at us while waving her arms. We put the bag back down, and my wife and I looked at each other in alarm, hoping we hadn't done something horrible, as the woman arrived, breathing heavily from her run.

"You don't have to pay the meter," she said and took a few gasping breaths. "The yellow bags. It means it's a holiday." A few more breaths. "You don't have to pay today."

My wife and I thanked her and as she walked away, I noted to my wife that back in California, most people would just laugh and think we were dumbasses who didn't know what they were doing. If a random stranger was willing to help us out before we even left our car, we figured this might be a good place to make our new home. Even though we hadn't settled there in Golden, I still remember that woman's kindness.

Done reminiscing, I checked online, looking for some sort of place that had psychic services. There were quite a few with decent reviews and one especially caught my eye. It looked like they acted as a "venue" for different seers who happened to be visiting the city. I could have been critical, but my mom's doppelgänger from New Orleans had definitely shown me a thing or two. I knew there was a chance I would feel conned, but also a chance that I would find something different, so I went.

It was a cool little shop, not too far from one of my clients. It had everything you would expect. No shrunken heads, but they had all of the crystals, yoga mats, and books on energy healing you could hope for. Oh, and a really weird cat.

What's with me and cats? I don't know. Maybe after naming our cat Chuck Norris, all of them seem a little more awesome.

I walked in, doing my best to stick out like a sore thumb, just like I wanted. It didn't take long before one of the clerks came up to nervously ask if there was anything she could help me with.

"I want to get a reading from whomever your current house psychic is," I told her, and her face winced a little bit. She told me she would look into it and went back behind the counter.

The Best ~ Miss Merideth was available. That's what it said on the sheet she handed me as she started to give a short bio and a rundown of her fees. I said she sounded just fine, and the nervous girl guided me back.

The room at the back of the shop was a lot like the room where my mother's twin had worked her magic. I walked through the lacy hippie drapes and started to take stock. There was a middle-aged woman in the room, watching me as I walked in. And there were cats. Two of them, in fact, sitting on a shelf and studying me from their perches.

"Welcome," she said, gesturing. "Take a seat and let's get started on what brings you here."

I had tried last time to throw the seer off, and it hadn't worked... at all. So this time around, I was ready to get to the point. I just wanted to clear up whatever was bugging me inside. I wasn't sure what to expect. Maybe, I was about to be told the most profound thing of my life. Maybe, this was just my way of going to the psychologist on the cheap.

"So, what can I help you with today?" she asked. At that point, I got a rather acute case of verbal diarrhea, and started to lay it all out on the line for her. I explained that I felt an internal block and that I wanted some "otherworldly" insight. I told her about the other seers I had been to. I told her about what they had said, and how they had done the reading, from tarot cards to my son's southern drawl. I explained that I wanted some help from whomever it was that was supposed to be watching over me, and would love a little direction.

When I finally finished my long mind dump, she waited a moment, as if expecting more. Then she said, "Perfect."

I took a deep breath and she said, "Have you ever heard of a chakra, and how it relates to you and the things within your sphere of energy?"

I was clueless, and the first thing that went through my head was a song from Chaka Khan, the singer from the eighties. But I had just embarrassed myself enough, so I squeaked out, "Sure. Of course, but tell me more."

I could lie and tell you that I remembered everything she had said about the Indian spiritual rituals and practice involved with chakras, but the truth is that I didn't catch a whole lot, and anything remotely detailed that I wrote here would be straight out of Wikipedia. So instead, I'll give you the short of it, as I understand it.

Basically, there is energy flowing through your body that helps you feel good physically as well as mentally or spiritually. Sometimes you get a kink in the hose, and that causes the energy to clog. It's like when people tell you that you're bottling up your anger, except with chakras, that energy is literally stopped. Luckily for me, there are people who have abilities that allow them to see where you are bottling up, and how to release those emotions. All for a price, of course. I'm not sure that I buy into all of that and it could just be a one-way ticket to con town.

"Wow," she stuttered, as if seeing me for the first time. "You have an incredibly light chakra. There is a lot of positivity in your life. In fact, the only real dark color I can see in you is near your throat, which is a darker red. It feels like anger that you need to find a release for."

I still wasn't sure that her entire interpretation was correct, but I was willing to try out her advice to see what I could get from it.

"It's not much of a clog, but there is definitely something making you angry. Not physically, but it seems like there is just something that you need to get out. Does that make any sense?"

It didn't make sense. It might have been related to the chaos in my life when I lost my job a couple of years back but for the last twelve months, everything had finally gotten ironed out and life and been on the upswing. So no, it didn't really make sense.

"Ok," she said, trying to move on, "I just have to tell you, I have done a lot of chakra readings and the amount of positivity you have flowing through you is pretty rare. I can see that you have a very kind heart, and other than the little bit of red, you have an excellent aura."

In other words, I just paid this woman to tell me that I'm a living incarnation of the Love Boat.

It was right then that the cat (you remember him right? Because I certainly didn't) jumped right up on my lap.

The embarrassment from the seer was palpable. "Oh, I am so, so sorry," she said. "Shiva, please get off that poor customer!"

"No, it's totally fine. I have a cat of my own," I said, thinking about Chuck Norris. "It must smell him on me or know I am cat friendly."

"Ok. He usually isn't even in here. He tends to ignore my clients when they come in. Just push him off if you need your space. After just thirty seconds of me petting him, Shiva sauntered back up to her perch to watch again.

The seer spoke up again, and said, "I have to tell you, as I was reading you and the things around you, I want you to know that you are very, very protected."

She must have sensed my disbelief of what she was saying.

"I just want to say that you have quite a few guardians around you. And, I'm getting a sense your mom's father has a significant presence around you. Does that make sense?"

Now she was just pulling the feel-goods out of her bag of tricks, trying to find a trigger. I guess it was my own fault for paying for this psychology appointment. It felt like it was turning into a game of twenty questions to try and cleanse me.

"Not really," I said. "I knew my father's dad, but not in great detail. My mother's father passed when I was four or five. I barely even remember him. I know we were always up at their place in Whitefish, but do not recall any real connection with him."

"Hmm" she said. "I really feel that he is with you and that he's here for a reason. Interesting you did not have a close bond. Well, he is here with multiple others as well. I don't necessarily think that they are related to you. Just fellow helpers. I also get that there is a huge presence with them. Yeah. You have a huge, friendly angel in your midst. I see a huge, huge man, with very brightly colored feathers and lightly colored garments. I know this person. I can't say off the top of my head. But someone in your midst really has been watching over you."

I had to stop her so we could chat a little more. I then told her that while I have my religion, I don't really practice it very regularly on any level. I appreciate aspects from all religions, and while I was born into a Catholic family, I really grew up more agnostic. So the talk of angels around me really wasn't making too much of a connection.

"No, no," she said, "I just report what I see and feel. Interesting... you should know that those that are around you know how you feel. In fact, they all say you identify more with the spirituality of Buddhism. That's what I see around you." She paused for a moment and then said, "Oh wait, I know who that is now. Sandlephon. Do you know of Sandlephon?"

"Not at all" I told her. I knew a few things about the bible because of my desire for self-education, but I was woefully inadequate at best when it came to religion and theology.

"Well, look into him," she said. "He is somehow connected to you and helping, or watching your path.

"Now let's take a look into your future. Ohhhh....OK. So here is the deal. Your work is satisfying and actually going very well, no issue at all there."

Her guess was spot on, but then I had already said as much.

"Yet, I am seeing something coming in the very near future for you. An opportunity. I don't have a read on exactly what it will be, but it will be a huge opportunity. A year from now, or within that range, this opportunity will present itself. You have to listen. It seems it will be given to you for a reason. I can't say whether it's something you take, or just something you have to listen to."

At this point, I mentally paused for a second. Now I have two seers in a row that were predicting some sort of movement in my work life with actual dates. That's a little odd. I can't help but hope she's not just playing the odds against middle-aged white men in polo shirts like mine.

"Well that is interesting," I said. "You see, I actually love my new job. It's a great company and it's actually challenging me more than I ever have been. That challenge is what keeps me creative, on my toes, and just generally interested. I really don't see myself leaving but then, I always listen, because you never know. So I guess, maybe?"

"Yes," she said, working it. "That's the thing though. This feels like a very creative alternative that also will challenge you. But, in a completely different way. I don't know. It feels like a new venture. I am so sorry. I feel a good read off you but all this is probably not making any sense to you."

The con was laid on pretty thick at this point. There had been a lot of blind, generic leading. It felt like a sales pitch, trying to find the right information that would get you a satisfied customer. I was starting to feel really conned... right up until I remembered something else.

"I guess it could be the fact that I started writing my first book," I said hesitantly. "I wanted to write something for my wife and children. It has become a labor of love, a gift of love punctuated by many short stories and thought-provoking themes. A love letter of sorts told through all of my eccentrically odd stories. I had hoped it would make them happy, and give them something to learn from my stupid, crazy decisions. I just wanted them to love life and all the little signs it gives you."

My mouth was running again, but I needed to get this out.

"I also needed to document some of these insane stories that my closest friends and I have been involved in. Time is not exactly on my side. Soon enough, the players in all the chapters won't be around to help me remember all of the details. I wanted to get these stories to paper so I could remember, and so my kids will know these stories of mine.

"I started letting people read some of the work-in-progress chapters, and people really started to like them. So I figured I might as well throw it out in the market to see if I can at least recoup the cost of writing it. And just maybe, someone out there will pick it up and it'll help them out or entertain in some way. What a wonderful feeling that would be."

She waited a moment before answering.

"Thank you for sharing," she said, large eyes shining. "I really think that you need to finish that book and do exactly what you stated. It could lead to something, but only if you choose that route."

I took a moment to breathe. Then, a thought came to me: now it was my turn.

In the previous three experiences with the fortune tellers, I let them do their thing. It was almost always different. But, now I wanted my turn. I realized that maybe my blockage had something to do with not having some answers. There were some things I just wanted to get off my chest. At worst she would just say, I don't know.

"Ok," I said, out of the blue. "I have two basic questions for you. They are ones that I have wanted answered for many years, and now more than ever."

"Sure. I will see what I can gather for you. Fire away."

I smiled my biggest smart-ass smile. This would end the charade or nothing would. While I have appreciated the nice words from the different seers, I wanted to see the *real* power. Actually, if I was telling the truth, I was more than hoping that she would get the answers wrong.

"First," I started, "Who took the bracelet, and why?"

She didn't even miss a beat. She closed her eyes and started moving around. The cat had decided to come down and sit on her lap. She opened her eyes and told me something strange, that my wife and I already assumed, but that no one else could really know.

"I see that it was a coveted piece by you and your wife. I know it had a lot of sentimental value. I see someone from your wife's side of the family. Someone with incredibly grey... no, white hair. But... it's not grey because of old age, but white because that's just its color. And, she says that she just wanted you guys to know she is still with you. It was an act of fun and kindness. I also gather this person was always into being fancy. Sorry, no name. But I feel she is a Grandma."

As she explained, I could feel my face go from that smart-ass smile to shock, and then to tearful gratitude.

We always suspected that her Grandma (her Dad's mother), whom I never got the chance to meet, was always with us, ever since we received one of her glamour paintings gifted to us at our wedding. It's a family tradition to hand down this portrait to the newest family member to get married. In it, a younger version of grandma is posing, near nude, in exotic lingerie, doing her best Marilyn Monroe pose. While everything is in full color, there is one piece devoid of color. Grandma's hair is snow white. Guess it always had been.

We loved that painting and hung it proudly in our first apartments and then our house, before we had to pass it on to her brother.

My wife had always felt her presence. We kind of thought it was her, but of course had no way of knowing. That is, until I walked into this random art-and-sage store and sat down with my fourth Seer.

There is no way she could have gotten that many specific things back to me that are so close to what we already suspected.

Maybe it's time to admit to you that I do kind of believe in this stuff. At least I have always been open to this sort of witchcraft, or whatever they call it. I mean, my mom's doppelgänger was more than enough to convince me to believe that maybe, just maybe, there are some people out there with the gift of the third eye.

"Well. I have to tell you," I said, shaking it off, "I am a little relieved. You see we always assumed that it was my wife's Grandma. We know there was no evil intent. We also believe the two children we lost before the two we have now are also part of that equation. I mean, we could hear children's footsteps all around us. It was weird, but I guess it brings some relief as well."

"Oh, they are with your Grandma. She is their protector. I do not know what you believe about the afterlife, but I truly do get that coming through. That energy is there."

I won't lie. That would bring a little tear to anyone's eye, and a tiny little squeeze of the heart. It did to me.

I sniffled a little bit and said, "Ok. Second question. Who was the man in the white pants? The man who I believe tried to do something to myself and friends when we were younger and to my sister when she was also younger."

She shifted back into her trance-like state and did some head-rolling. Shiva decided it was my turn for some lap time and sauntered over to plop down on my lap.

Finally, she came back and glanced back and forth between me and the cat.

"It's the same man," she said, a little confused at first. "It is one hundred percent the same man. He hurt many others in his life. There are more that people do not even know about. I know he is no longer around and I know that he is no longer a threat to anyone. I also get his name is a common name. It starts with a…W…yeah. It's like Waylon, no… more like … Wayne."

The blood completely drained from my face. The cat must have sensed the hairs stand up on the back of my neck, because she decided it was time to go back to her overhang perch above us.

I was dumbfounded. There was just no way. I hadn't given her any information when I walked through that store door. No credit card. No license. No address. I told the girl at the counter my first name and she walked me straight back to get my reading.

There was simply no way that she could have known that his name was Wayne. The odds of that were astronomical.

But then, who am I to say what is or isn't possible? I've been struck by lightning twice, I won the lottery with my wife and kids, and I have repeatedly been in horrible situations that should have had dire consequences, only to find that life is constantly getting better. If I've learned anything, it's that my life is more than just a set of probabilities. And now, I had been handed on a silver platter the answers to two of my strangest yet most spectacular stories.

"I can't actually believe you *named* the guy I always suspected," I said after a moment. "That is such a huge relief. That clog that was blocking me? The one that was making it hard to get from one day to the next is gone. Thank you so much, not only for your kind words and friendly cat, but just for being able to help me out. I truly do want to give that back to the people around me and maybe to others."

We chatted for a little longer before I finally left, feeling grateful and at peace.

I can't say that you, dear reader, are going to run into the same things that I have in my life. No one's life is exactly the same. I can tell you that the lessons I've learned are not unique to me. The little coincidences add up. You might be surprised at how random little acts led you to where you are today. If you look, they are there. Those big signs I was looking for? I don't know that I ever saw them, but I think I had my eyes opened up to all of the small signs that follow all of us from day to day.

I'm still not sure where they come from. I don't know how to explain them. I invite you to be open to them, regardless of where they come from. If an opportunity comes your way, be willing to entertain it. If you start something new, don't expect anything from it. Work hard for what gains you earn in your life. Never give up.

Hell, it took me thirty years to get definite answers to two of my *smallest* questions.

I have one last piece of advice when it comes to seers: Don't go back to the same seer twice, and even then, be very careful. Sometimes you may not want to know the future. Sadly, not every future is rosy. Sometimes though, your future is very bright.

No matter how hard it gets, no matter what life throws at you, whether it's a serial killer, a lightning bolt, or just a poor decision, always remain positive. It will help you wade through the pain of everything that doesn't really matter, and help give you a different perspective. Not every choice you make will be correct but in the end, we'll all be there to help guide and help keep you safe. Even if you don't know it's us.

"I'm learning to fly, around the clouds." —Tom Petty

Chapter 24

Madame Vera

Estes Park. There was something about it the first time we ventured up there. Specifically I think it was the town's world famous marker: The Stanley Hotel. An impressive feet of engineering and construction that still stands to this day. Also what the world knows as the inspiration and backdrop to one of the most famous novels written, The Shining.

There is such a special charm when you venture up the mountain to what once used to be a sanctuary for people suffering from tuberculosis. The altitude in Estes is already impressive. When you are sitting on the mountain looking down at its charming bustling little city and the Rocky Mountain National Park in its background, it is breathtaking to say the least.

It was one of those must stay places. And many, many years ago, before my wife and I had kids, we did just that. It was a grand piece of history that we gladly partook in the group led, paranormal history of The Stanley Hotel. Drinking with your best friend and going ghost hunting? How do you say no to that combo? Needless to say, while the tour provided much color and history to the place, and the secret location of the pet cemetery, it did not provide the scares. We even ventured out late at night to see if we could catch a glimpse of Mr. Stanley from yesteryear, to no avail. Still. Amazing place to take a long weekend and decompress with life slowing down and worries washing away.

The best part of that weekend, which was about twelve years ago, was the basement tour. That's supposedly where most of the ghost activity occurs. It's also where they have a awesome little Stephen King shrine of personally signed novels to the staff and management of Stanley. But there was also something else that caught my eye. So much so that it has been imbedded into my brain to this day. And no, I did not see a ghost. Not that day anyways.

I saw, on a snowy, random Saturday the name of a person I knew that I needed to visit with. Or at least someone I would see in the future. The sign was over a darkened hallway door and simply read: Madame Vera. And as not to confuse the point, there was sign in the other glass window that said: Resident Psychic. Something told me right then and there that not only did I need her to read my future, I just simply needed to meet this human. Can't quite explain that and still can't. Was just an internal feeling. This was also only after number one and two psychic stories above, so my belief of the ultimate con was still ingrained in my head.

As it turned out, Miss Vera was not around and wasn't taking appointments. Not a big deal. I would simply return another day and handle my inner unknown need. My wife just gave me the "sure" look. Next time. Sure.

Lo and behold we did come back, almost yearly in fact. Summer and Winter; both glorious times to visit that little slice of heaven, always missing Madame Vera. About our fourth or so visit I finally got a glimpse of Miss Vera. She was just about to start a session with a client. From the distance, down the hall, she looked every bit the part of a psychic. Long grey hair with an upscale dress and presence about her. Unfortunately, she was finishing up after this client and we needed to go back home. It wasn't meant to be. At least yet.

We had a hectic travel and life schedule the next couple of years. It was time we just didn't have to take some leisure fun in Estes Park. So when we finally did make it back up, the city was as vibrant as ever. Although I swore to myself I felt something missing. I would soon find out what it was when we took our typical visit around The Stanley. The old building stood glorious in its spot. But we saw some major construction happening around the hotel and in the front court yard. When we got parked and started our roam up to the hotel, we saw they were developing a new building. A building that would look exactly like The Stanley, except smaller, less rooms. They were expanding. And they were designing and digging the new bush maze (copied from The Shining), straight out of the movie. Such an awesome idea.

As we made our way into the hotel I made a B-line for the basement. This was it. I was going to catch Vera at the right time. I had to. But I couldn't find her door. They had turned that part of the basement into a coffee / bakery place. I stepped down to the other side of the basement. Nothing there. Just the old haunted workers' tunnel and management office. Vera was MIA.

I asked the front clerk what happened to Vera. She had no clue. She was new and had heard Vera hadn't been there in a while. I left Estes a little befuddled that I missed my window on someone I knew I had reason to speak to. I was a little bummed, but had hope she would show back up. I was hoping she did not leave our plane of existence.

For the next four years I would always check. The signs on the doorways would always remain the same, unchanged. Then about two years ago, on a random bathroom break, I caught a glimpse of something new that wasn't there on our last visit. It was familiar and yet new. On the end of the opposite hallway of Vera's old office, was her new office. Just like that. Six months later. The Resident Psychic sign was there, but the office was blacked out. No one was home, but she had cards outside her office now. I took one and saw her phone number. Perfect. I would now be able to book it on my own. Besides, I had a new psychic story under my belt. A crazy meeting with my mom's long lost twin sister. I wondered what Vera would pull out of her hat. I still had that feeling that I had to visit with her.

But I didn't. All sorts of life, some of which you have read above, got in my way. I didn't make an appointment and when we were back in Estes, much less now with new kiddos, we just didn't have time for me to be gone an hour or so. Every sort of reason, but she was still there; how long, who knows?

And then a confluence of events sent me the earthly invitation I needed. I had visited a fourth psychic and gotten some interesting info. But that psychic was different than my mom's mirror. I needed to see this Madame Vera as it had been 12 or more years since I had that knocking feeling in my head that wouldn't go away.

I was a mere month removed from the last psychic I had seen. I felt less of a stress on me but I still knew there was probably something I was missing. Also, if you couldn't tell, I am someone that is always in need of a new adventure and a new perspective in life. I was also leaning towards the fact that I was ok with the con that was going on. Still. Those specific predictions from the last two psychics had got me thinking.

The other path that presented itself was that it turned out the new company I was working for had business in and around the area of Estes Park for me to attend to. Path A was merging itself with Path B. This time I didn't hesitate. I found Vera's card in my work desk. I called the number. No one answered; I had to leave a message for Madame Vera. What the fuck do you leave a message about to a psychic? I mean, shouldn't they technically already know that I am calling and why? Totally joking here. That's not how it works, but one would think that it should. I simply left my first name and number and then politely asked her to call me back. Then I got busy and forgot about it.

When I saw the caller ID the next morning say Estes Park, I knew right then who it was. Vera. She was very happy for nine in the morning, she greeted me like an Aunt that hasn't spoke to her favorite nephew in a few months. She proceeded to tell me she keeps limited hours and is out of town quite a bit. I assured her it was no issue, I just had her info and was reaching out for a session with her. She was a very direct, to the point lady. She asked why I wanted to come in. Just told her I had her info for a little while and I always wanted to chat. I didn't have anything that I really needed to address. She said absolutely no issue and we booked a later afternoon session a few days in advance. I had to be up there for work so it all just fell into place. Where as I had been apprehensive, almost cynical in the prior Seers' sessions, I was genuinely happy about finally getting to meet someone I subliminally stalked for almost twelve years. Or maybe I was just happy that indeed she is still alive.

I'll admit something here. I had a random thought about how I originally planned this chapter. The title of the original chapter was supposed to read "The Easiest Chapter I Ever Wrote," and it would only contain a URL. And that URL would lead the reader to YouTube. You see, at the foot of the stairs that led down to meeting one of the coolest people on the face of this earth, I decided to do something I had wanted to do at my last four sessions: have a physical record of my encounter. And I could. Colorado is a One-Consent state. As long as I consented, I am allowed to record a conversation. I wanted it for my own personal recollection, if there was any way it was going to end up like the previous experiences.

I pushed record on my phone app and headed in to listen to my destiny. Possibly. There can always be a trick in there somewhere. Luckily I found out quickly that not only was my twelve year itch correct, but I was in for another interesting revelation.

But that's a story for another day, and another book. Plus I have to give it time to gestate to give Madame Vera the chance to prove her ability true. I wouldn't want to jinx the awesome information that I got from merely stopping in to say hi.

Cheers!

Dedication

This book is dedicated first and foremost to my wonderful children. This book is dad's love letter to you both. Avoid the stupid pitfalls in life and navigate the big ones with ease. Hopefully this dumb ass roadmap helps weave that better in your futures. Notice Mom is missing? She knows this has dedication to her as well. But the reality? She's the subject of, and dedication in, the third book of this trilogy. I love you three like Ron Burgundy loves Baxter. Like that old couple in *On Golden Pond*. Like those damn dogs in *Where the Red Fern Grows*. Like Jack loved Rose in *Titanic*. Undying, loyal, ignorant, without a second thought, pure love. My choices have always played a role in shaping me. They will for you as well. But I also know, without a doubt, that we shaped each other. You working on me just as much as me working on you.

To answer your questions:

Yes, your dad was a jackass.

Yes, these stories are all true.

Yes, I almost made the mistake of not taking a chance on the greatest human beings on earth.

Yes, technically, I was sometimes not on the "right" side of society (spoiler alert, no one is). But, I made myself productive. I did some things, then did some even cooler things. I will continue to do even more cool things, with you guys, of course.

And, I have made my way this far. And that was quite a feat.

Do not be scared. Always go forward, even when it hurts. This too will pass. Let go of anger as soon as possible; it's a deterrent to everything. Always call, text, video, brain implant (or whatever you use in the future to communicate) your parents. We love you more than you know.

Be a good person. Detract from the gossip, bullying and general negative vibes. Live life to the fullest. Enjoy everything, but moderation is a must. Trust me on that. I've seen a thing or two.

Read. Write. Always challenge yourself. Celebrate your successes, even the small ones. Make a point of doing random acts of kindness to strangers (R.A.K.S.). Never let emotion dictate decisions. Never let alcohol dictate decisions. It's even worse than emotions.

Buy your mom wine and flowers whenever possible. Always buy your dad a beer and a meal, and a house on the lake, and maybe a few vintage cars. I think I might be getting carried away here.

Just be your already-awesome-selves, and take the time to do some extra here and there. It pays dividends. It has on my nine plus lives.

Acknowledgements

This book would not have been possible without my wonderful family and friends, living and dearly departed, in my life. They have helped guide me and console me. They have helped me make some bad choices and overall gave me the zest for life that has led me to this very day.

To my wonderful parents and fantastic siblings

Thank you. For not killing me in so many situations that we all found ourselves in. Plus, you know, being the "oops" baby could have gone so many different ways. You have always been there to listen to my bullshit, to help guide me through my bad decisions, and have had undying love for my wayward friends. You did well Mom and Dad!!

To my wife

You are my rock. Things are not perfect and they never will be. Our lives together and these stories are evidence of that. But we have always pushed past the bad and fought for the good together. For that, and everything else, I am grateful beyond words. Oh, and thanks for that other thing! Super cool! Seriously though. Never moving to Miami, without you.

To my kids

Other than me telling you this, you will never truly know how much you shaped and guided me out of some dark times. You both are so extremely independent, smart, and beautiful. You have been nothing short of a miracle. By the time I actually let you read this, I know you will be well past the teen years and already headed to adulthood. Stop. You will get to be an adult soon enough! Seriously. Enjoy being a kid. You will miss it when you are older or, you will follow in my footsteps and keep that "inner" child in your heart and wear it on your sleeve throughout life. Never let anyone or anything dictate who you really are.

To my friends

Many of you have stuck around for over thirty years now. I know as we have gotten older, taken on more responsibilities, and been geographically further apart that it has been a struggle to fully keep in touch. That too will change and come back full circle. I never see myself without any of you. You are my extended family. I am so proud of each of you. The struggles and the obstacles that each of you have had and yet each of you are still prospering! You are a proud bunch. Keep up the good fight!

To my readers

My new friends. My new fans. And all my good old buddies. While I started this little journey as an ode to my wife and kids, I soon realized that others could possibly benefit from my insights and stupid decisions if nothing more than a simple laugh to get you through the day. This is not rocket science here. But, it does lend itself to provoking you to think about your past. Mistakes are beautiful things. They help guide you to a better place. Never be ashamed of who you are or what you have done. Own it. Fuck what "others" think. Always take it as constructive criticism to only yourself.

P.S. There are little morsels throughout this book that could, if you try hard enough, lead you to the real Chance. Just a fun extra I wanted to include as I love puzzles and quests. Shit. My life has been nothing but one large side quest. Bet you can say the same about yourself! Cheers!

About the author

The author of this book you are reading has been the subject of many layers in life. Love. Happiness. Relationships. Paranormal. Unbelievable. Just dumb luck. He happily resides in a small mountain town, close to the hustle and bustle that all of us endure in our lives. He is happily smitten with his lovely wife of twenty years, who spends her time nurturing and coaching the future leaders of this free world. They have two little beasts that like to suck the time and money out of them. But they would not change it for the world. This world is what we all live and breathe in. It is up to us what we make of it and how we look at it. The author is exploring his own reflection of the world with the hope to get you, the reader, to view your world with a little more compassion, a little more humor, and most importantly, with an open mind.

www.ingramcontent.com/pod-product-compliance
Lightning Source LLC
Chambersburg PA
CBHW031423290426
44110CB00011B/499